THE BOOK ART
OF
LUCIEN PISSARRO

THE BOOK ART
OF
Lucien Pissarro

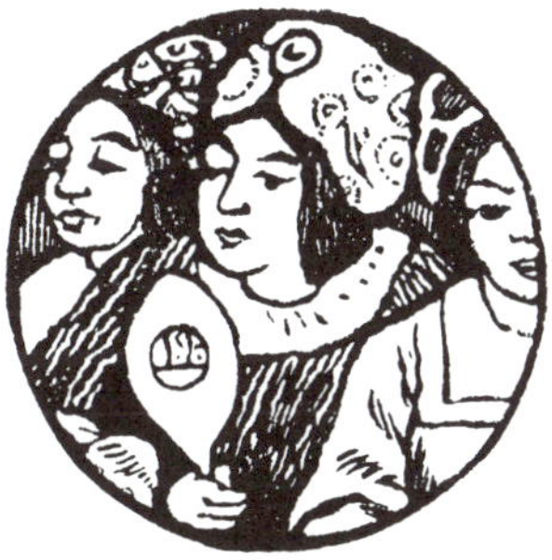

WITH A BIBLIOGRAPHICAL LIST
OF THE BOOKS OF THE ERAGNY PRESS
1894–1914

LORA URBANELLI

MOYER BELL : WAKEFIELD, RHODE ISLAND & LONDON

For Will, my dear companion

LIBRARY OF CONGRESS CATALOGING-IN-PUBLICATION DATA

Urbanelli, Lora S.
The book art of Lucien Pissarro / Lora Urbanelli
128 p. cm.
1. Pissarro, Lucien, 1863-1944 —Themes, motives. 2. Illustration of books—19th century— England. 4. Ergany Press. 5. Wood-engraving—England-Oxford. 6. Ashmolean Museum. I. Title.
NE1149.5.P57A4 1997
769.92—DC20 96-18095
ISBN 1-55921-191-1 CIP

Printed in the United States of America

Distributed in North America by Publishers Group West, P.O. Box 8843
Emeryville CA 94662
800-788-3123 (in California 510-658-3453)
and in Europe by
Gazelle Book Services Ltd., Falcon House,
Queen Square, Lancaster LA1 1RN England 524-68765

CONTENTS

THE BOOK ART OF

LUCIEN PISSARRO

LUCIEN PISSARRO, first son of the Impressionist artist Camille Pissarro, was a gentle man, shy and very quiet. Despite these qualities, and the clamorous orbit of artists around his father, Lucien grew to find his own voice. Under Camille's very loving – but somewhat overbearing – watchful eye, he found his place, not among the great painters of Paris, but in England during a private press revival, which he not only helped to shape, but to which he made serious and unique contributions with his Eragny Press. Indeed, Lucien brought together, in a way that no one else at the time was able, the avant-garde ideas of the Parisian Neo-Impressionists and the rich tradition of English Arts and Crafts publishing embodied in the work and life of William Morris. The resulting synthesis, so graphically evident in the evolution of Lucien's wood engraving style, was completely his own.

Born in Paris on February 20, 1863, Lucien spent his first twenty years moving with the family, a group consisting of both parents, one surviving sister and four brothers.[1] As his father and the Impressionist painters struggled for recognition, the Pissarro

1. In the following biographical sketch, as well as for general inspiration, I am indebted to Alan Fern and his unpublished dissertation "The Wood-engravings of Lucien Pissarro with a Catalogue Raisonné."

I would also like to acknowledge the work of Marcella Genz, whose recent doctoral thesis in Library Science, "A History of the Eragny Press 1894–1914," includes a very useful clarification of biographical facts and an excellent analysis of the business records of the press.

family's financial burdens grew. Moving intermittently from Paris to Pontoise, Louveciennes, Britanny, London (during the Franco-Prussian War) and back to Osny, Camille rarely sold a painting in these years, and when he did he was forced to compromise on its price. The tenacious painter was a man of extraordinary artistic principle, however, and greatly respected by his colleagues. Moreover, he was a doting and devoted father and, though failing at the business of art, an admirable role model for the growing Lucien.

Notwithstanding the disapproval of Madame Pissarro, who would have preferred that her children, especially her eldest, learn a more lucrative and practical trade, Camille encouraged Lucien to focus his attention on art, to relentlessly study and draw from nature and to cultivate his painting skills. They frequently went on painting trips together, a practice that continued all their lives. Not surprisingly, Lucien's artistic approach derived from the elder Pissarro's and from a young age he painted in the Impressionist manner.[2] Later both men explored the scientific precision of Pointillism, conceived by their young friend Georges Seurat and the other Neo-Impressionists. Lucien, in a modest act of independence, remained true to the Pointillist technique throughout his life, despite his father's eventual dismissal and derision of it.

Lucien inherited more than a keen eye from his father. His lack of concrete business skills and, indeed, his disinterest in acquiring them, was evident from Lucien's first job in 1878 at age fifteen and did not substantially improve with maturity. In 1883, nearly five years later, Lucien was sent to London to live with his uncle Phineas Isaacson; his parents, especially his mother, anticipated that he would overcome his shyness, improve his English, secure permanent employment, and perhaps augment the family income. While the first two objectives may have been met, the

2. For a complete catalogue raisonné of Lucien Pissarro's paintings, see Thorold, *Catalogue of the Oil Paintings of Lucien Pissarro*. The catalogue raisonné of the artist's prints is in the final stages of completion by the author and Alan Fern.

latter two were certainly not. He was, however, exposed to some great masters and, despite his mother's attempts to steer him otherwise and his father's weak efforts to concur, Lucien seems to have made the decision at this time to dedicate his life to artistic rather than business pursuits. Perhaps the most important realization of this trip, however, was the beginning of a lifelong rich and revealing correspondence between father and son.[3]

> Osny, March 15, 1883
>
> My Dear Lucien,
>
> You do indeed show strength of will in harnessing yourself to English, nothing but English. . . and your future, too, who knows? — do not give up drawing, draw often, always from nature, and whenever possible consult the primitives.— If you could only be persuaded that no other activity is so intelligent and agreeable. What would be perfect would be for you to become quite mad about art; Sundays and holidays would then become days of real happiness — you would await them with impatience. . .[4]

As this brief passage indicates, Camille's message was a mixed one: Enslave yourself to your senses, but, yes, try to reserve art for the weekends!

During his year abroad, the young Pissarro was surrounded by the people and the ideas that would shape his future as he toyed with concepts that he would later develop. He traveled with his cousin Esther Isaacson, his future sister-in-law, and discussed their mutual interest in Socialism. Through the Isaacson family he met his future wife, thirteen-year-old Esther Bensusan. He worked without pay for a music publisher, and studied diligently in the galleries of the British and South Kensington Museums. Lucien's letters home included enthusiastic descriptions of

3. See Rewald, *Camille Pissarro: Letters to his Son Lucien*, 1943; and the recently published Thorold, *Letters of Lucien to Camille Pissarro*, 1883–1903, 1993 (hereafter referred to as *Letters*). Also, Bailly-Herzberg, *Correspondance de Camille Pissarro*, in five volumes.

4. Rewald, *Letters*, p. 24.

the great marbles, Chinese porcelains and Holbein drawings which he examined there.[5] He actively exchanged his own drawings with Camille, who in return sent Daumier prints to inspire him and special papers on which to work. One such paper was for "gillotage", a photomechanical means of reproducing drawings for journal illustrations. Although Camille disapproved of the popular process, it is clear that both men were thinking of ways for Lucien to combine art and commerce.

At home that summer, Paul Gauguin visited and painted with Camille. They discussed the concept of producing Impressionist inspired tapestries, pottery and fans as a way of disseminating their own art to a wider audience. At this time, a revolution in the industrial arts, one which considered everyday objects in terms of satisfying design and careful craftsmanship, was already under way in England, thanks primarily to William Morris, and repercussions were beginning to be felt abroad. Lucien's letters from this period, however, made no mention of this movement which eventually was to have such a lasting effect on him. After a brief visit home, during which he went on painting excursions with his father, Lucien finished out his year in England, and finally returned to France in March of 1884 to help the growing family settle into their new house in Eragny sur Epte.

The following six years for Lucien, until his permanent relocation to England, were vital to his artistic development. During this period he divided his time between Paris and Eragny. While in the country he painted with his father, experimented with etching and, inspired by his discovery of the work of Kate Greenaway and Walter Crane, designed and illustrated chil-

5. *"J'ai vu à South Kensington des meubles extraordinaires. Il y a entre autre chose un meuble renfermant un panneau lequel est fait de petits morceaux de bois de differentes couleurs et plaqués représentant des figures, on pourrait faire des sujets modernes dan ce genre, ce serait vraiment revolutionnaire. Il y a aussi des porcelaines de Chine magnifiques, je me demande comment ils font pour avoir des tons aussi puissant."* As Thorold points out, Lucien would later be inspired by figures such as these found on Asian pottery and fashion them into wood engraved illustrations for Nerval's *Histoire de la Reine du Matin*, 1909, and Gautier's *Le Livre de Jade*, 1911. Thorold, *Letters*, pp. 31–33.

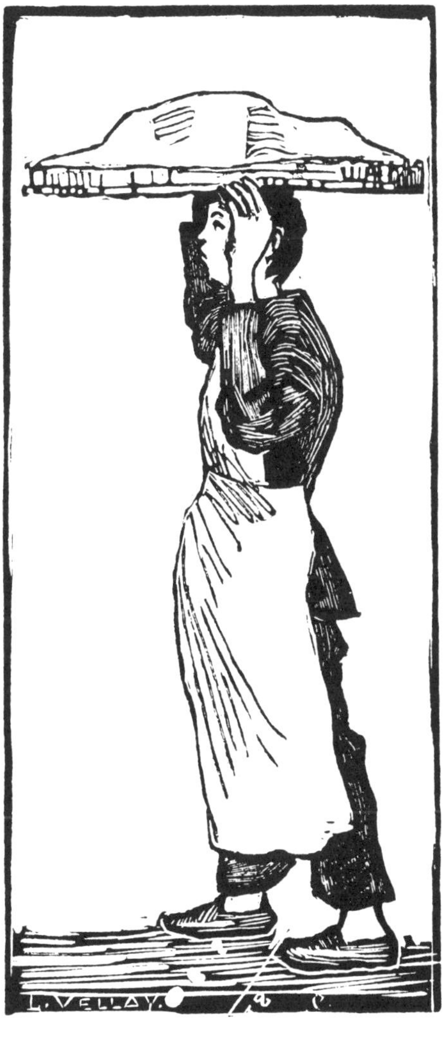

Figure i
Le Pâtissier
c. 1884

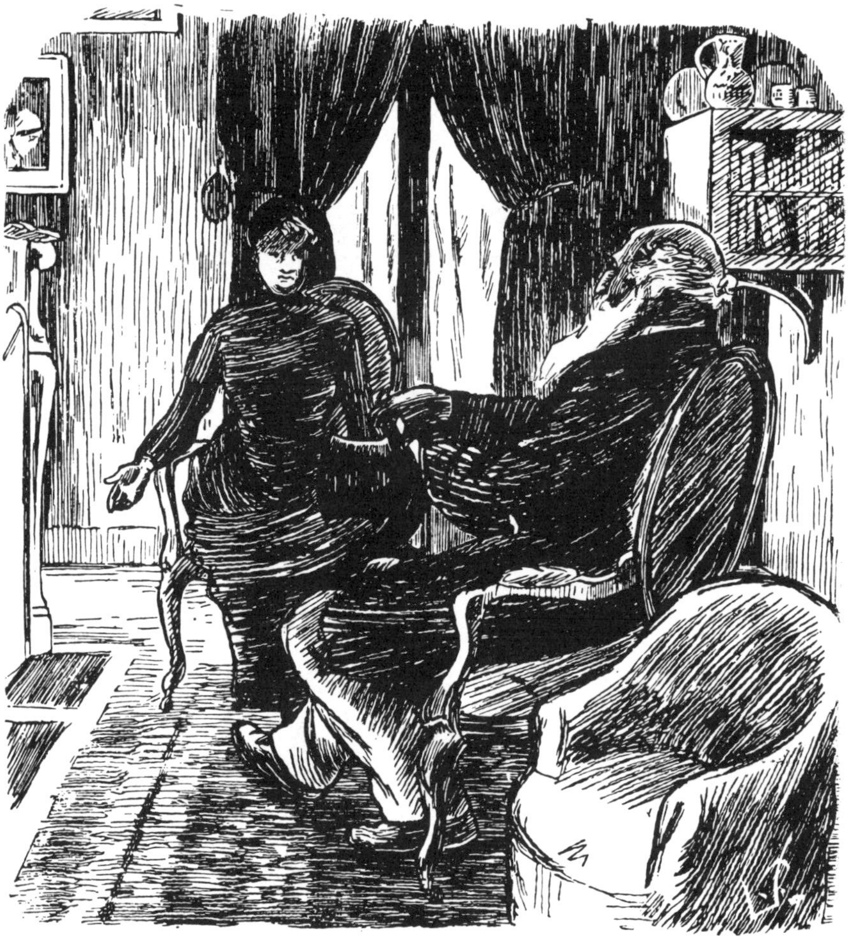

Figure ii
La Visite
c. 1886

dren's stories for his younger siblings. In Paris Lucien obtained a job with the firm Manzi for which he worked making plates for color printing,[6] and studied the proper art of wood engraving with August Lepère. To his great credit, Lepère was careful to emphasize the non-commercial aspects of the medium to his

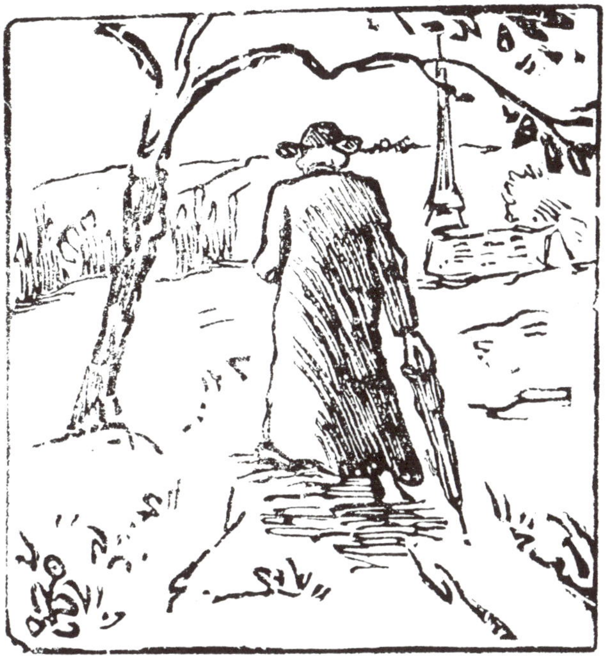

Figure iii
Le Curé
c. 1885

young student, despite his own reputation for slick presentation.

In the wood engraving "Le Curé," from 1885[7] (Figure iii), Lucien shows his early concern for reproducing the exact appearance of his drawing on the wood. In essence denying the strictures of the medium, he cut the image to the contours of his pen line, and created an effect more like a woodcut (removing wood around the line) than a wood engraving (incising the block to cre-

6. As quoted in Fern, p. 22, Lucien felt that the instruction gained at Manzi was essential to his later mastery of printing wood engravings in color.
7. The work is signed "L. Vellay", Mme. Pissarro's maiden name. He used this alias for a short time at Camille's advice, in order not to be associated with his father, who felt his work to be too unpopular with the buying public. According to the notebook in the Pissarro family archives at the Ashmolean Museum, this work was published in *La Vie Moderne*, October 1, 1887.

ate a white line). This approach to the block would change dramatically over the next decade.

In 1885 Lucien and Camille began to associate with Georges Seurat, Paul Signac and Félix Fénéon, whose interests ranged

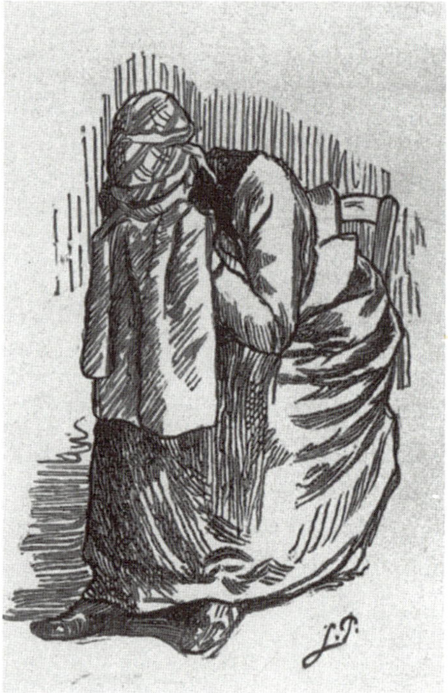

Figure iv
Mirbeau
Les Infortunes de Mait' Liziard
1886

from social anarchism to the development of new theories in color perception which would later be termed Pointillism and Neo-Impressionism.[8] With support from his father and these new friends, Lucien began to seek out a means to publish his drawings, whether in the form of children's book or as illustrations in any of a multitude of contemporary French publications. In the former quest he was frustrated; in the latter, he enjoyed mixed success. The most important commission for Lucien at

8. As noted earlier, both Camille and Lucien began to paint at this time in the Pointillist technique. Camille abandoned the method in 1890, finding it too restrictive. Lucien, when he painted, continued throughout his life to apply Pointillist principles.

this time was the illustration of Octave Mirbeau's "Les Infortunes de Mait' Liziard" published in *La Revue Illustrée,* June 15, 1886. Although well received among friends, the work was considered too unpolished by the reading public, accustomed to a more refined presentation. (Figure iv) Lucien's drawings and wood engravings appeared intermittently over the years in *Le Chat Noir, La Vie Moderne* and, starting in 1890, in the anarchist journal *Père Peinard.*

In the meantime, quite independent of his father, the younger Pissarro's stature as an artist was beginning to grow. He began to exhibit paintings, drawings and prints on a regular basis in, among others, the eighth and final Impressionist exhibition (1886), the second exhibition of the *Société des Artistes Indépendents* (1886), with *Les XX* in Belgium (1887) and in *Les Peintres-Graveurs* at Durand-Ruel (1889). His work, especially his wood engravings, was well reviewed.

By the end of the decade, Lucien had become more engrossed in making prints. Indeed, it was only in the medium of printmaking that he finally acquired an independence of style and expertise. Even so, from the time that he began learning to print, Lucien worked at the task of reproducing his father's drawings. Both men spoke often of collaboration, especially as Lucien's knowledge of color printing became more sophisticated. Their first joint project was not to see fruition until 1893,[9] but Lucien's body of work began to reflect this mutual desire, despite his inability to find financial backing. Moreover, his love of children's book illustration was finding no custom in Paris. Both father and son began to realize that perhaps the only way for Lucien to take advantage of his developing skills and to reach his aspirations was to live

9. *Les Travaux des Champs,* published by the Vale Press in 1893, consisted of six wood engravings by Lucien after drawings by Camille. Three were single color; three were printed with up to six blocks of color. See below p. 22. Lucien did not complete the larger, more complex collaborative project that he wanted to in Camille's lifetime. "*La Charrue d'Erable*", perhaps Lucien's *tour de force,* was not published until 1912. See below, p. 33.

and work in a more congenial atmosphere. The position which England held in support of the decorative arts was well known. The Pissarros were also convinced that the English public was more receptive to the graphic arts. After a visit to London in the spring of 1890 with his father and the artist Maximilien Luce, it became clear that if Lucien wanted an independent career in his new found *métier* he would have to leave France. That November Lucien moved to England permanently.

Within a few months of his arrival Lucien began to move in the circles of those artists who were shaping the private press movement. If one were to date the onset of this movement, it would have to be two years earlier with a lecture given at the first Arts and Crafts Society Exhibition in London (November 18, 1888). Entitled "Letterpress Printing and Illustration", it was delivered by Emery Walker, a friend and neighbor of William Morris, and relied heavily on Morris's own collection of 15th Century illuminated manuscripts for its lantern slides. Already a noted proponent of the aesthetic re-evaluation of shoddy, mass produced household goods, Morris also championed reform of the social and industrial systems which had alienated craftsmen from their product in the first place. His devotion to what became the Arts and Crafts revival motivated him to set up his legendary crafts workshop. By the time of Walker's lecture, Morris had also been experimenting with book design through the Chiswick Press, a commercial operation, as a means of publishing his own writings. After the speech, Morris approached Walker about his desire to design a new typeface to better suit his ideas, "to re-attain a long-lost standard of craftsmanship of book printing."[10] In 1890, inspired by the large lantern slide projections of colored borders and beautiful type, Morris succeeded in establishing his own press operation with his own typeface designs, which brought the craftsman, the artist and the printer together under one roof, the Kelmscott Press.

10. Roderick Cave, *The Private Press*, p. 104.

William Morris looked to Gothic design for inspiration when creating his books. The overall aesthetic product was heavy with decoration. He used special papers specifically designed to emulate 15th Century Bolognese papers, had gold specially hammered for his gold leaf, and encouraged British binders to produce a proper vellum for his covers. Although beautiful as objects of art, they were criticized by some as "overdressed", as books that asked to be looked at and admired, but not read.[11] The Kelmscott Press, however, was very successful commercially. Although only in operation for seven years, it became a large, profitable organization, ironically almost commercial in its production. In that short span the press produced 52 books in 66 volumes. Illustrations were provided by the artist Edward Burne-Jones and, although woodcuts and wood engravings were used in the production, they were all carved by a technician after Burne-Jones' drawings. Morris himself never printed at his own presses, but instead masterfully directed a substantial staff of others. William Morris died in October of 1896, but not before witnessing the great outpouring of interest in the book-beautiful that Kelmscott books had generated, both at home and abroad. Close associates Sydney Cockerell and Emery Walker carried on for eighteen months to finish out editions, but sadly, much was abandoned.

Just as Kelmscott Press was being established, Lucien Pissarro arrived on the scene. Thanks to a letter of introduction to the poet John Gray written by his friend Fénéon, Lucien was brought into the circle around Charles Ricketts and Charles Shannon, two young artists who hosted salon style gatherings at their studio in Chelsea named "The Vale".[12] These gatherings entertained the likes of Laurence Housman, Oscar Wilde, George Bernard Shaw, William Butler Yeats, Roger Fry and the painter William Rothenstein, among others. As a group of artists and writers their interests were varied, but they enjoyed engag-

11. Ibid. p. 111.

12. The Vale previously had belonged to Whistler.

ing in the polemic of reconciling John Ruskin's theories with more modern aesthetic concerns.[13] In this regard their interest in avant-garde art was very welcome to Lucien; in turn, they gladly received Lucien's introduction to French Symbolist literature. The Vale group was also interested in wood engraving as an art form and, in addition, was hungry for contact with other contemporary (read "continental") artists.

Ricketts founded the Vale Press soon after Kelmscott was under way and was unavoidably influenced by Morris's undertaking. Rather than look to Gothic design, however, he was more interested in the simpler early Renaissance books of Aldus Manutius.[14] Wishing to avoid what he characterized in Kelmscott borders as designs "full of wine", Ricketts proclaimed that Vale's books were to be "full of light."[15] In contrast to Morris's dense border vegetation, Ricketts's designs were cleaner and, as a result, his books more approachable. Vale books were printed at the Ballantyne Press and, like Morris, Ricketts chose not to be physically involved in that process. However, he was responsible for the first progressive step away from Morris by insisting that artists cut their own wood engravings for illustrations.

At long last Lucien's love of book making and illustration was to find fruition at the Vale through Ricketts's interest not only in making his own contribution to the private press movement, but also in publishing the work of other artists. *Twelve Woodcuts in Black and Colours by Lucien Pissarro,* frequently referred to as the "First Portfolio", was published by Vale in 1891, though not completed and distributed until 1893. It included three multiblock color pieces for which Lucien was beginning to establish quite a reputation. The five-color print "Le Fagot" (Figure v), actually began in 1889 while Lucien was still in France, was shown to the Morris circle by Emery Walker. Lucien reported to Camille that

13. Fern, p. 39.

14. A facsimile edition of Manutius' *Hypnerotomachia Poliphili* from 1499 had just been released in England in 1888. Darracott, *World of Charles Ricketts*, p. 37.

15. Ibid., pp. 48–49.

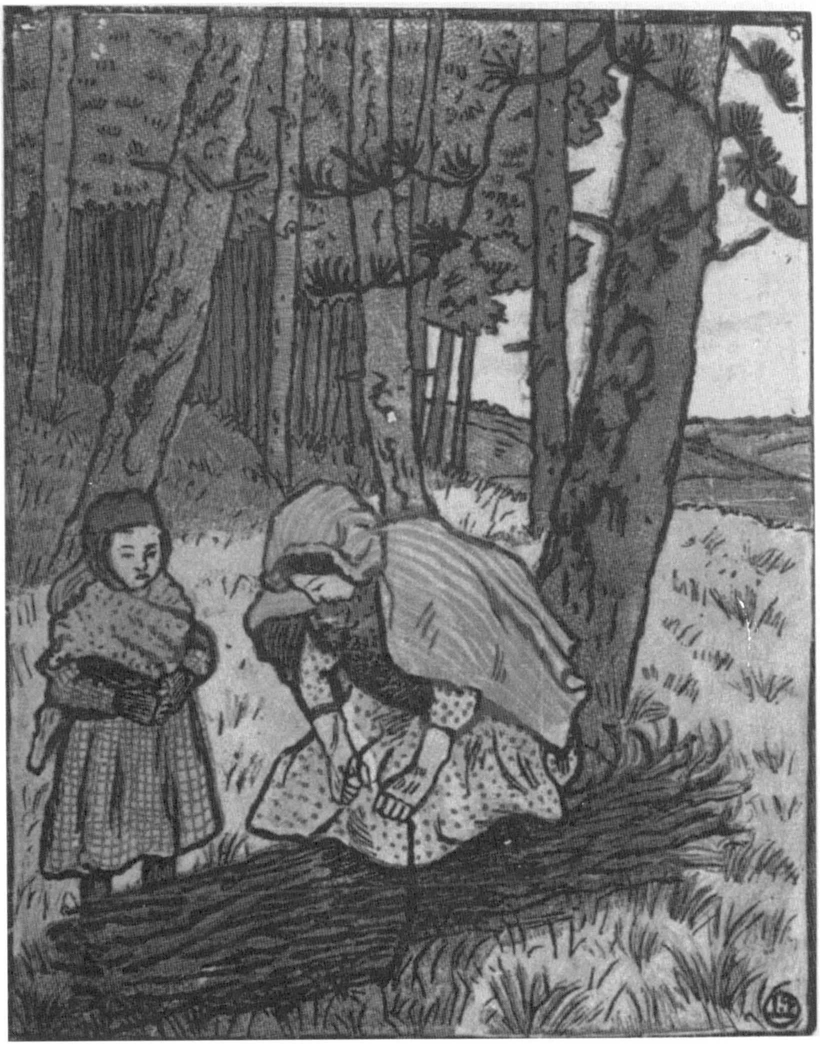

Figure v
Le Fagot, reduced
1889

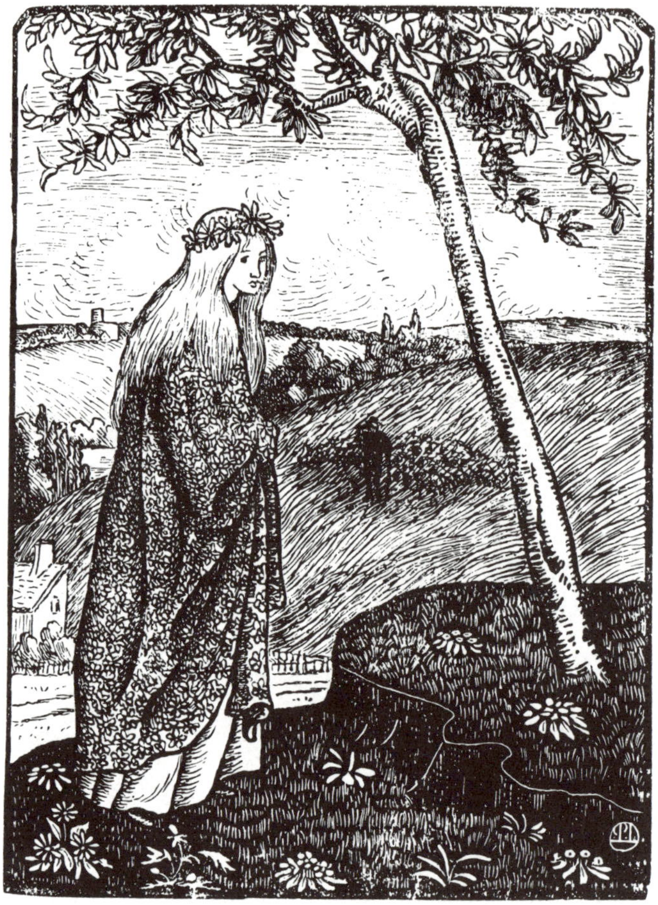

Figure vi
Sister of the Wood
reduced. 1891

they were very impressed with his abilities in color wood engraving, the likes of which they had never seen.[16]

Lucien was invited to contribute to Ricketts's occasional publication. *The Dial*, and did so in 1892 with his wood engraving. "Sister of the Wood" (Figure vi). Of this work Camille exclaimed: "Méfie-toi des préraphaélites!"[17] It is true that stylistically the Vale group had an immediate impact on Lucien, and his work did begin to show the influence of the Pre-Raphaelite artists Burne-Jones and Dante Gabriele Rossetti. But not having been trained in the English academic tradition, Lucien's work main-

16. Thorold, *Letters*, p. 169.

17. "Beware the Pre-Raphaelites!" Ibid., p. 200.

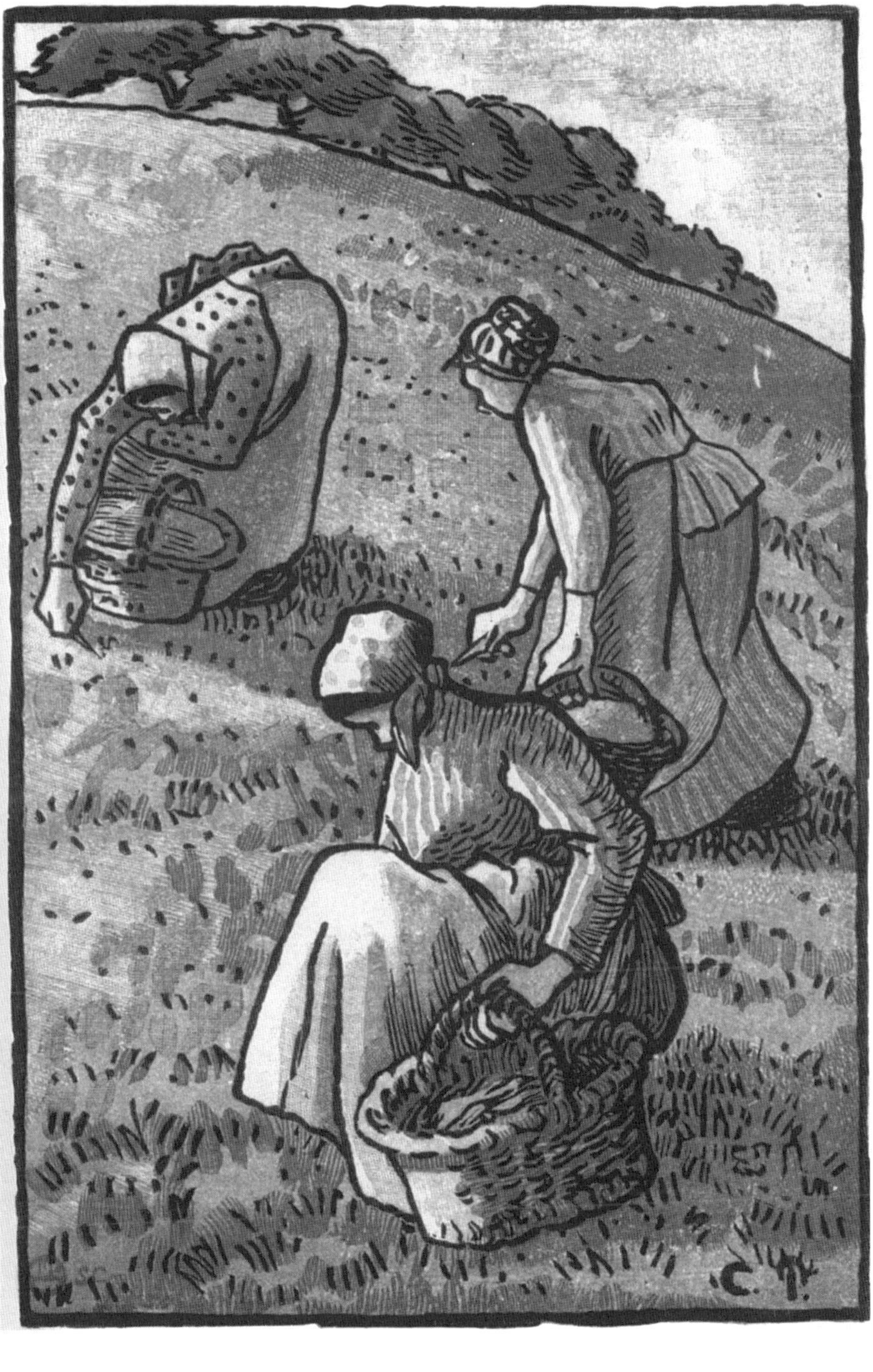

Figure vii
Femmes Faisant de l'Herbe
1893

tained a French character and a slightly naive quality, which his father urged him to preserve and nurture.

The following year a selection of Lucien's and Camille's collaborative prints was published by Vale in a small portfolio of six images. Entitled *Les Travaux des Champs*, and printed in an edition of twenty-five copies, the work was not a commercial success. That is not to say that the joint effort was futile. Particularly satisfying was the work, "Femmes Faisant de l'Herbe", a six-color block print showing each artist at his graphic best. (Figure vii)

Despite Camille's growing disquiet with his son's new friends, Lucien's association with Ricketts and Shannon gave him focus and provided him with career choices which were nothing like his father's. His stylistic explorations allowed him to begin to define himself and afforded him occasion to argue for that self-definition against Camille's better judgment. Equally as important for Lucien were the business opportunities that his Vale affiliation generated when he began to publish his own books.

In early 1894 Lucien wrote to Camille that he was busy at work cutting the blocks for a little book. He complained that the cost might prevent him from carrying the project through and, since it was something he had been working toward for so long, he hoped that perhaps Camille could afford to buy him a small press.[18] By now Lucien and his wife, Esther Bensusan Pissarro, and their new daughter, Orovida, were living just outside London in Epping (Essex) at the "Brook". With new equipment and space to set up a workshop, the Brook was the perfect place for Lucien and Esther to establish the Eragny Press, which they named after the Pissarro family's home village in France. Fortunately for Lucien, Vale's new partner, Llewellyn Hacon, agreed to handle the business end of Lucien's future production. For a percentage of sales, Hacon and Ricketts supplied ink and paper for

18. Ibid., p. 345. "*...Tu sais depuis combien de temps j'ambitionnai de faire un petit livre! A propos, je voudrai bien avoir une petite presse à main pour pouvoir faire le tirage moi-même et assez vite — si je trouv quelquechose de pas cher* [of course] *est — ce que tu pourrais me donner l'argent pour l'acheter?*"

the Eragny Press and paid any extra printing costs.[19] Eragny books were then distributed through Vale and marketed by John Lane at the Bodley Head; it was a happy arrangement for as long as it lasted.

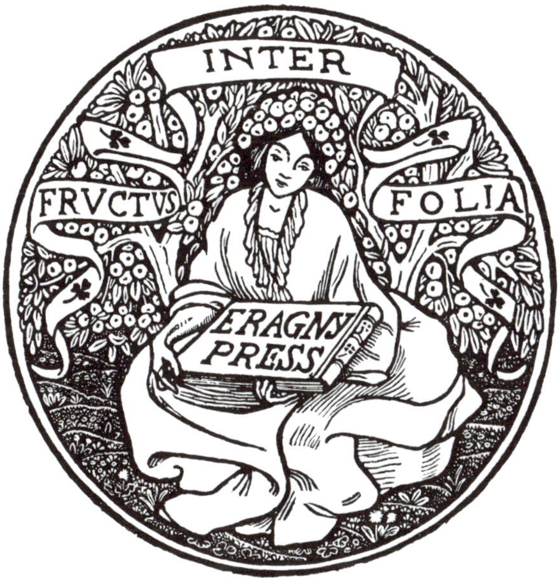

Figure ix
Pressmark
1899

That same year Lucien and Esther produced their first book with an Eragny Press imprint, *The Queen of the Fishes*. The story was an old Valois fairy tale which Lucien had been working on, in numerous versions, for many years. This final English interpretation, translated by Esther's friend Margaret Rust, was richly illustrated with color prints and borders and lettered with photo-engraved calligraphy for the text, which was printed in gray ink. (Figure viii) Lucien's involvement in every step of this intricate procedure allowed him to indulge in a true joining of letter forms and illustration, a dimension of design that would concern him for his entire career.

Queen of the Fishes was well received. As a first book it was

19. This and other details of the business arrangement between Lucien and Hacon & Ricketts are detailed in Genz, p. 95.

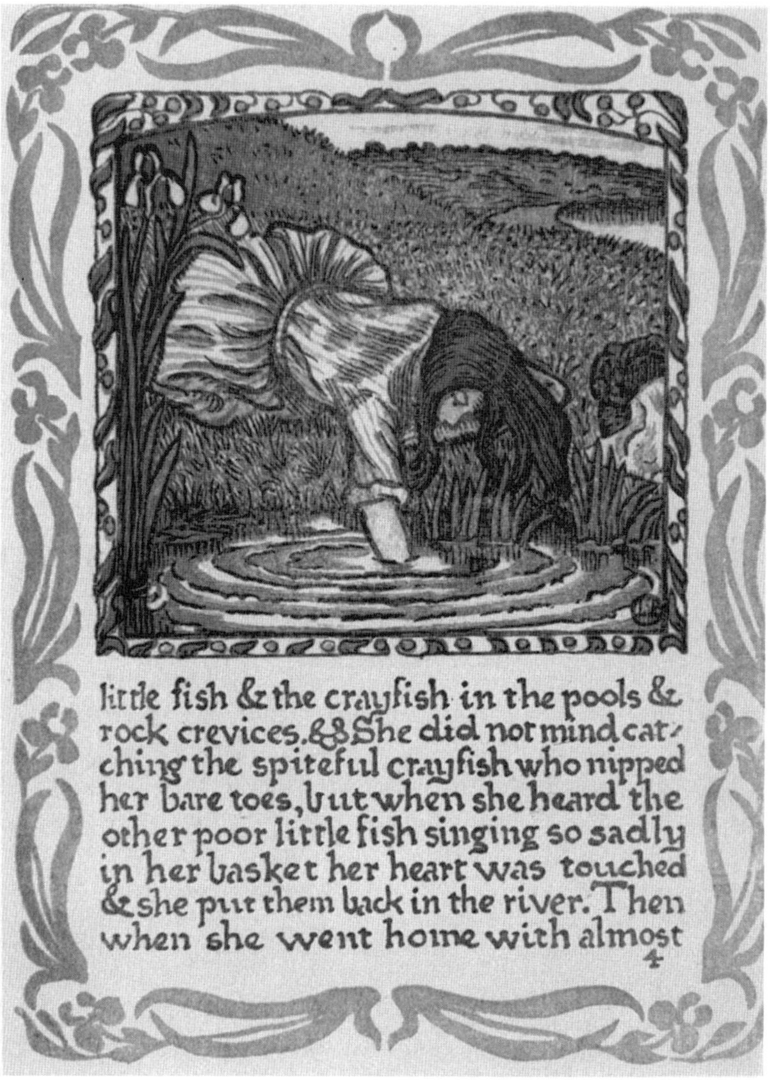

Figure viii
Girl reaching into a stream from *The Queen of the Fishes*
1894

rather experimental, and yet it maintained the *naiveté* and freshness of character that had so defined the young Lucien. Sigfried Bing, director of *Maison de l'Art Nouveau*, exhibited the work at his *l'Exposition Internationale du Livre Moderne* of 1896. Ambroise Vollard, who went on to become an important publisher of

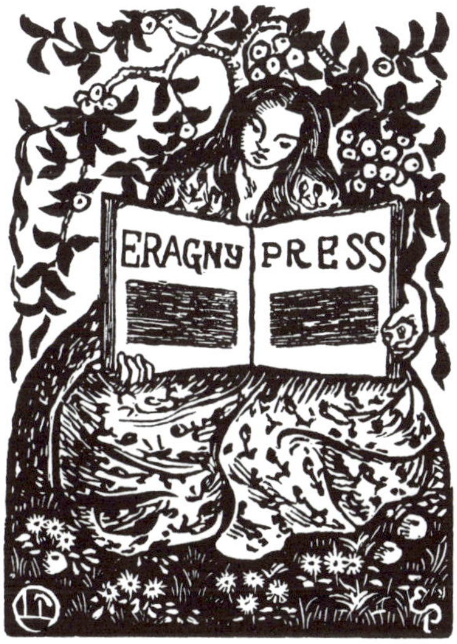

Figure x
Pressmark
1894

artists' books himself, said that at first he was disheartened by seeing this beautiful piece and wondered how anyone could top its perfection; but in the end, its beauty influenced his decision to go forward.[20]

Over the next nine years the Eragny Press continued its business arrangement with Hacon & Ricketts, who bought half of every edition outright and actually sold out one book before it came back from the binder.[21] This proved to be the most lucrative period of the press's twenty-year production, but in the end

20. Ambroise Vollard, *Recollections of a Picture Dealer*, p. 170. When Vollard did begin publishing, he asked Lucien to illustrate with wood engravings Paul Verlaine's *Parallèlement*. Camille, however, advised his son to turn down the offer, claiming that Vollard was far too demanding and did not pay enough. The book was eventually illustrated by Bonnard with lithographs. Una Johnson, *Ambroise Vollard*, p. 24.

21. That book was Perrault's *Deux Contes*

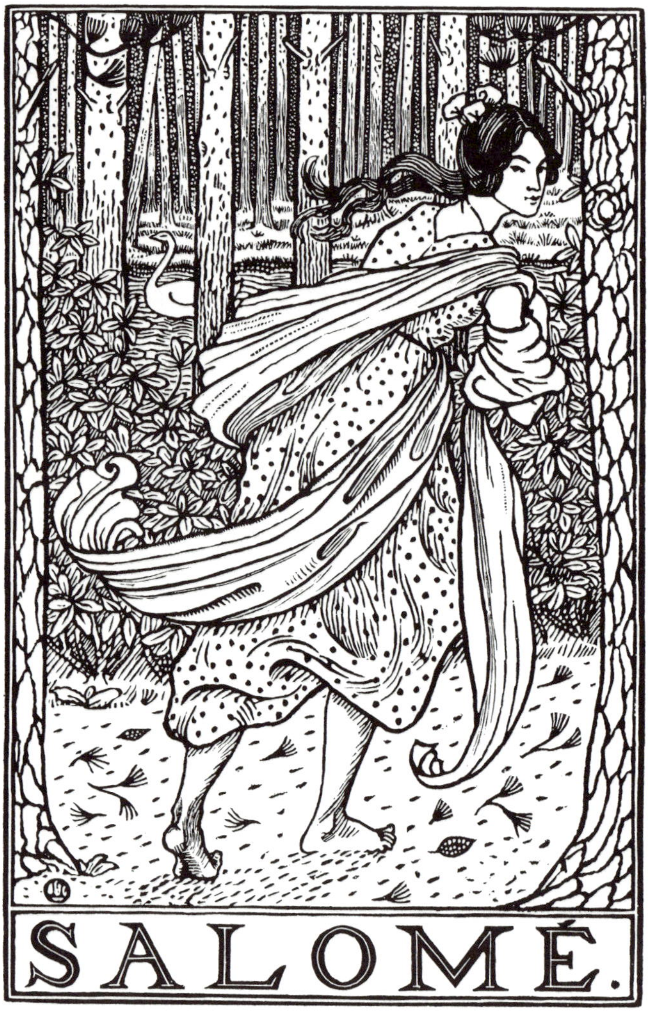

Figure xi
Laforgue
Les Moralités Légendaires I
1897

the operation was still not greatly profitable. Camille helped to finance the Press as much as he could until his death in 1903, but the younger Pissarros were always short of funds. Lucien, it seems, had learned a good but arduous lesson from his father: that artistic issues should always take priority over monetary concerns. Consequently, because of their high standards and production costs Lucien and Esther rarely made a profit.

The Eragny Press was truly a labor of love. Whereas Morris and Ricketts never actually printed at their presses, Lucien and

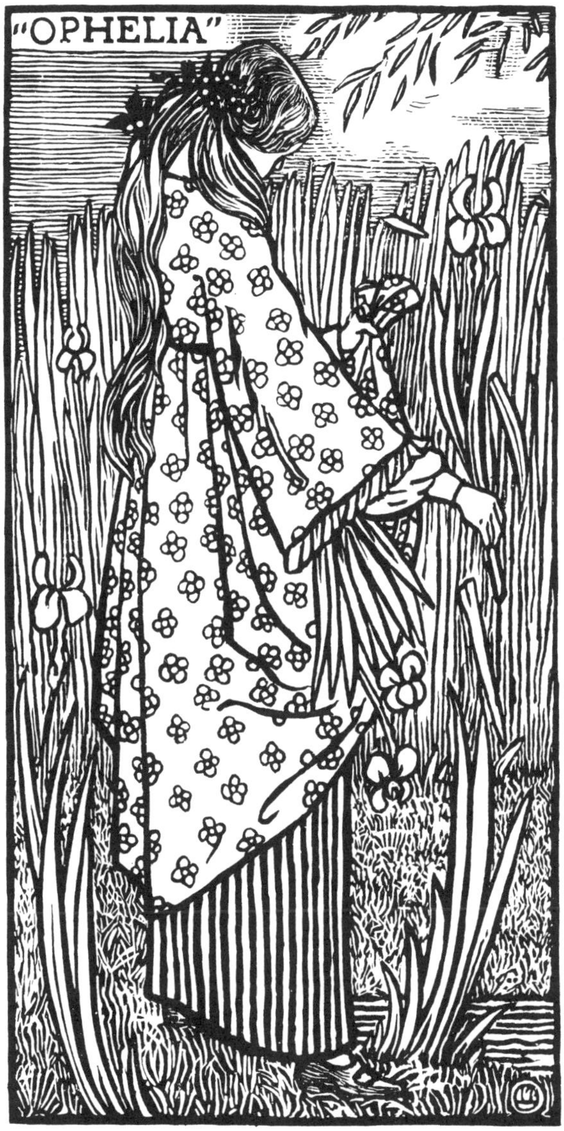

Figure xii
Laforgue
Les Moralités Légendaires II
1898

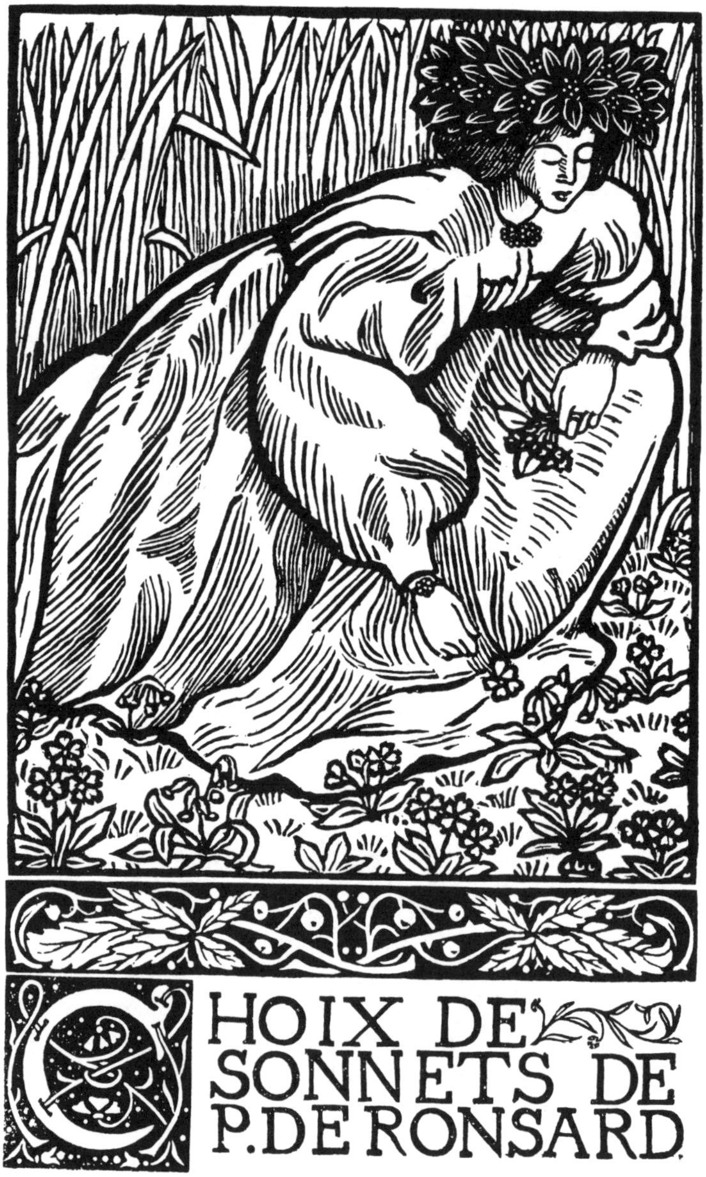

Figure xiii
Ronsard
Choix de Sonnets
1902

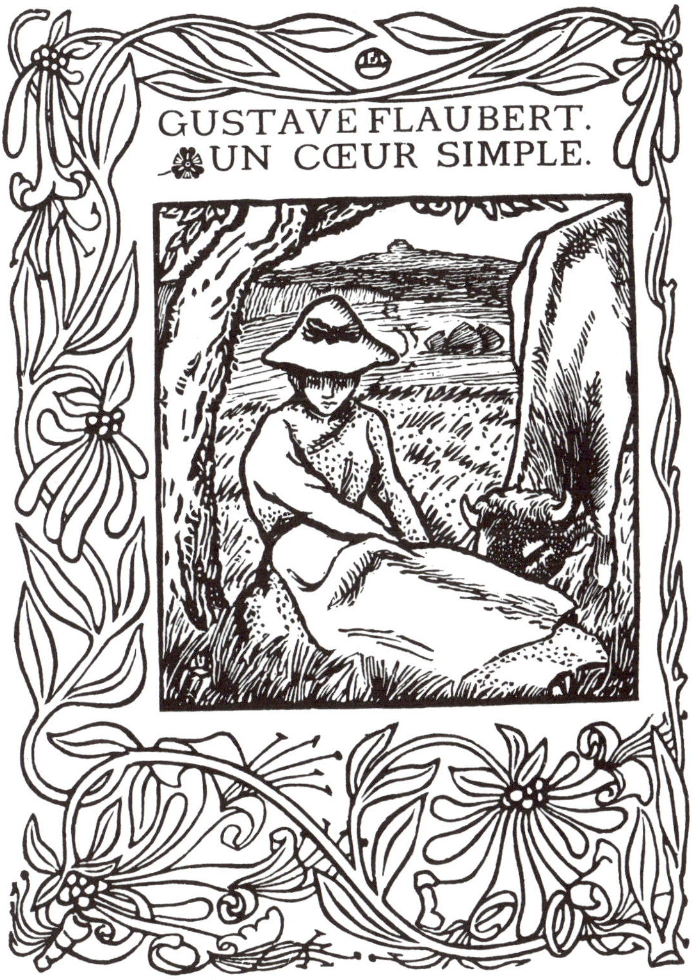

Figure xiv
Flaubert
Un Cœur Simple
1901

Esther designed the books, engraved all the blocks, set the type and blocks together, then painstakingly proofed and editioned all their work, occasionally hiring a printer to assist. Production was slow and their spoilage rate was high, especially when producing their later color work. However, it was precisely that immense involvement that made their books, above any other, the only "genuine Arts and Crafts product".[22] Their commitment was absolute and their methods meticulous and almost entirely self-taught.

22. Genz, p. 53.

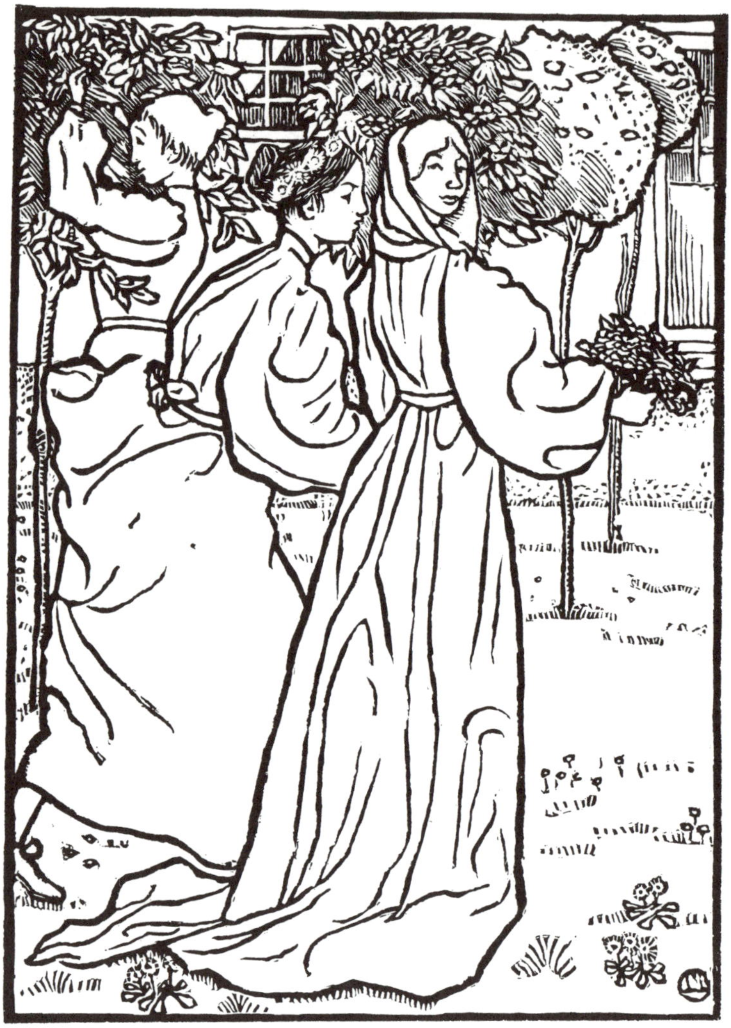

Figure xv
Browning
Some Poems
1904

Despite using photography to transfer his drawings to the block, Lucien's engravings developed on the wood as he cut them. Sometimes, the more decorative blocks were cut by Esther after Lucien's drawings, or they occasionally shared that task. Esther, an artist in her own right, was a strong and opinionated woman and very much a presence in every aspect of the business. Aside from assistance in carving, she helped with the proofing and the running of the presses. Esther may have even been responsible for the trademark flower-patterned paper covers of

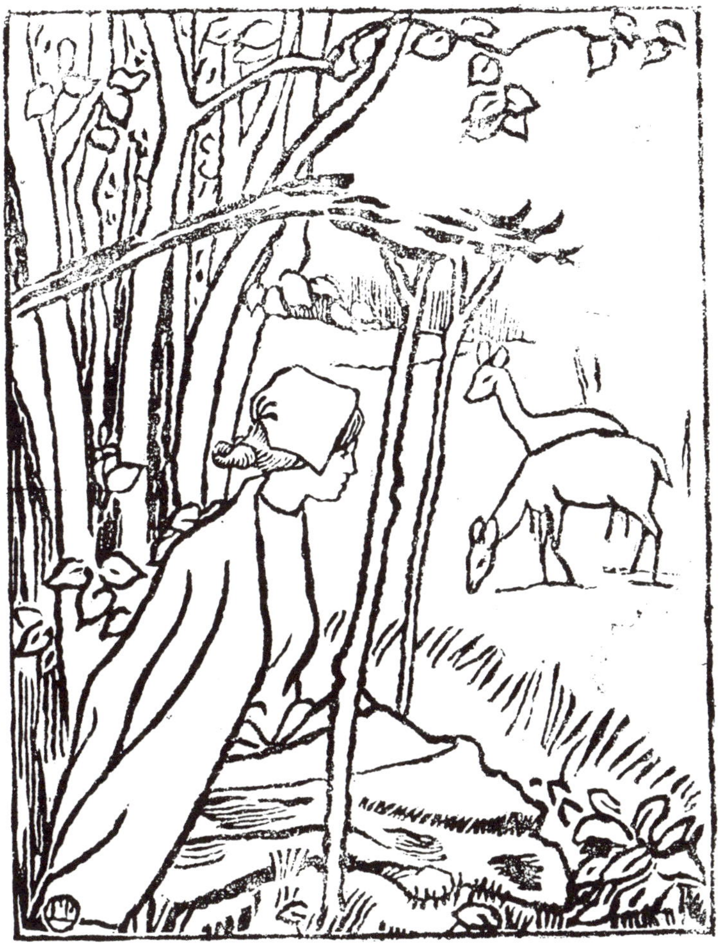

Figure xvi
C'est d'Aucassin et de Nicolete
1903

Eragny books, as she was also known as an excellent gardener who tended the enormous garden at the Brook. Her talents proved indispensable when, in 1897, Lucien suffered a stroke. It was two years before Lucien's health was finally restored, but the fingers on his left hand remained paralyzed. During this long recovery, Esther kept the press and the business active.

After *Queen of the Fishes*, the Eragny Press produced fifteen more books through the Vale Press. Thanks to Ricketts's generosity, the books were set in the newly cast Vale type and sometimes even used Vale watermarked papers. In contrast to their first book, this next group of works contained little color.

These books usually contained a complex frontispiece with an illustration, a border and decorative capitals. Aside from ornamental fleuron at the end of lines and sections, the rest of the book was often left unadorned. The vigorous black and white patterning of these designs was reminiscent of Kelmscott and

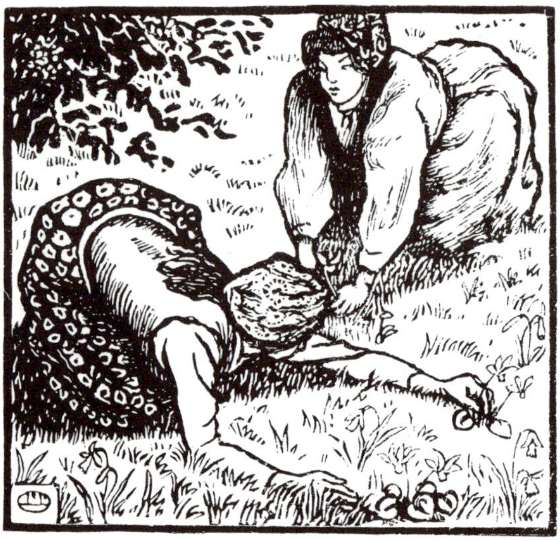

Figure xvii
Nerval
Histoire de la Reine du Matin et de Soliman Ben Daoud
1909

Vale books and reflected the height of England's influence on Lucien. Ironically, it was also in this distinctly Pre-Raphaelite period that many of the Eragny Press books were printed in French to attract continental collectors. (See Figures xi–xv) Overall, early sales were moderately successful.

In 1903 everything changed. In that year Camille Pissarro, Lucien's guiding light and lifelong confidant, died at age 73. As if that were not enough, the Vale Press closed its doors after a damaging printer's fire and never reopened. In one year the Eragny Press lost its two primary sources of financial and moral support. Luckily, the year before Lucien had finally finished the designs for his own typeface and Camille had subsidized the production of the matrices and punches. He called it the "Brook" type and his last sixteen books were published using it. Brook type was a lighter, more subtle version of Vale, on which it was based, and

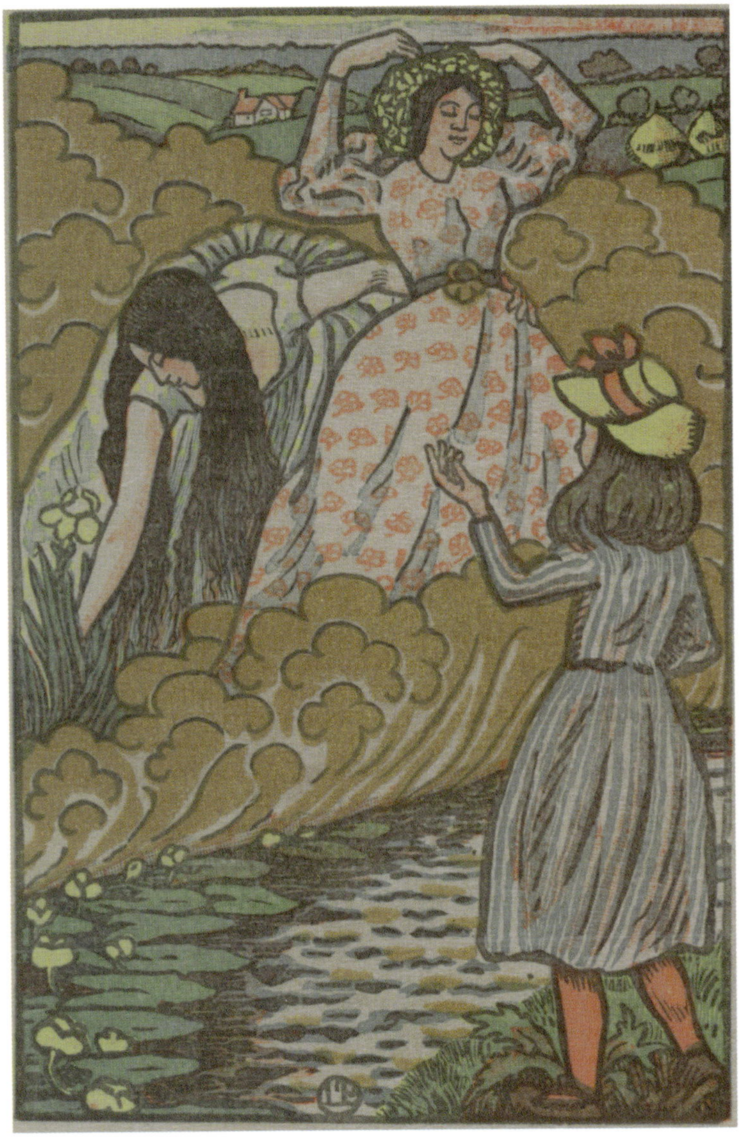

Rust
The Queen of the Fishes
1894

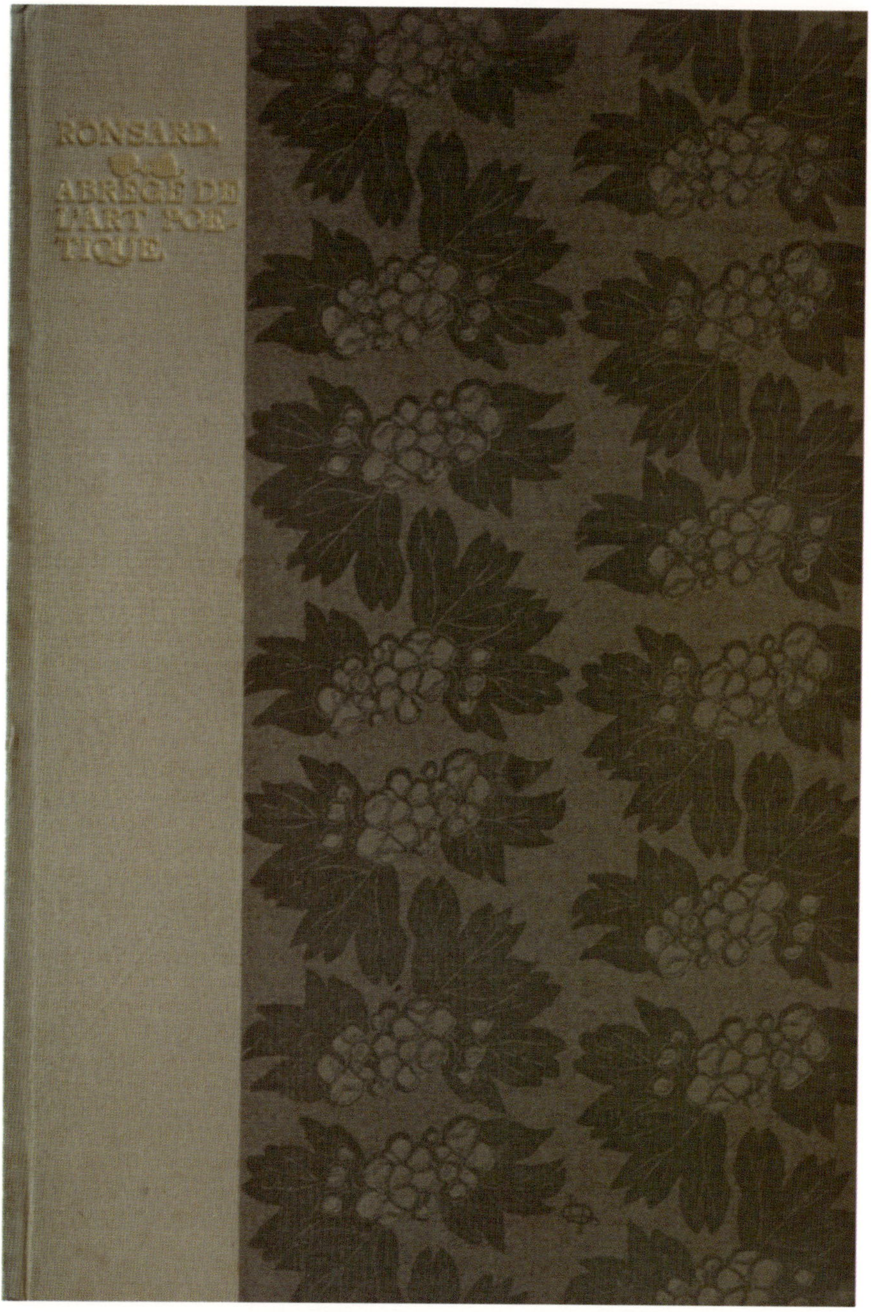

Ronsard
Abrégé de l'Art Poetique Français
1903

Bacon
Of Gardens
1902

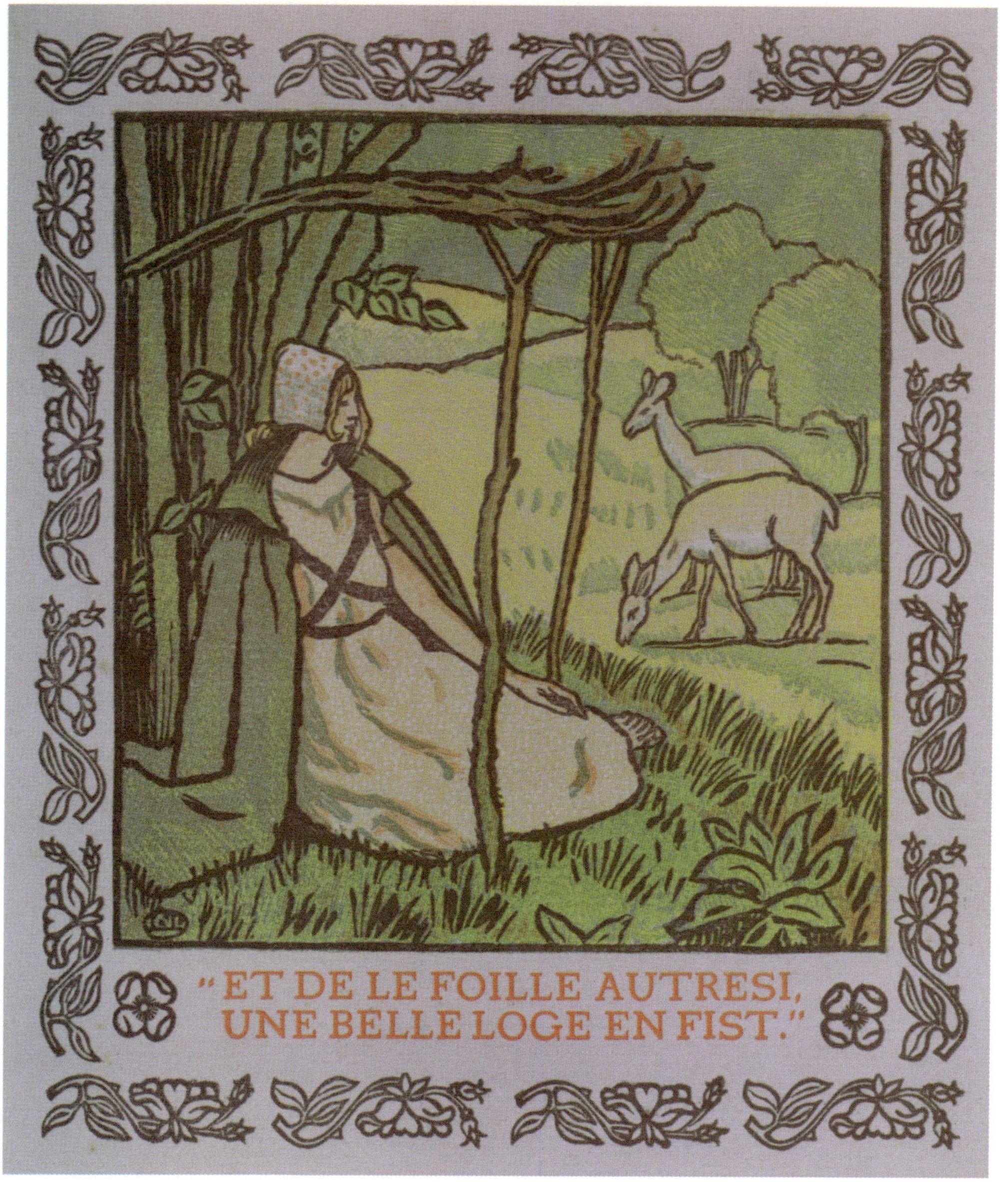

C'est d'Aucassin et de Nicolete
1903

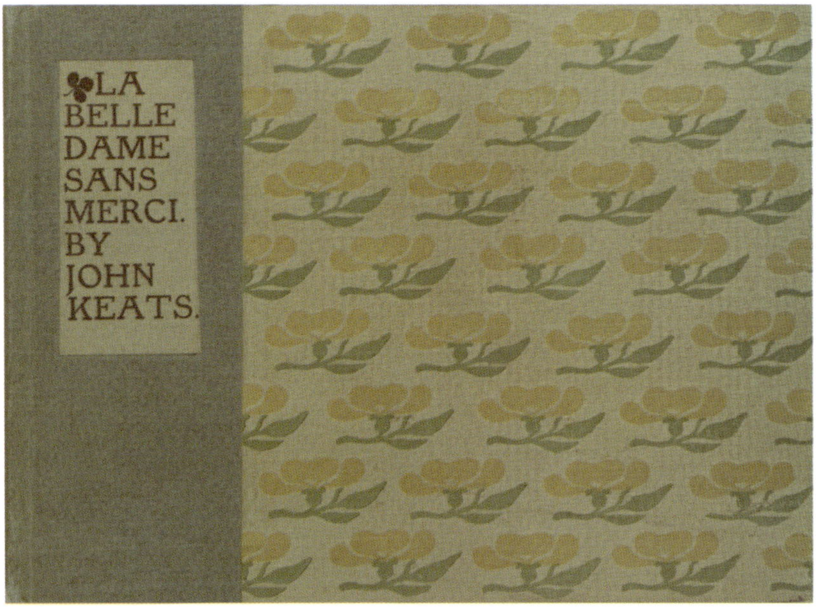

Keats
La Belle Dame sans Merci
1906

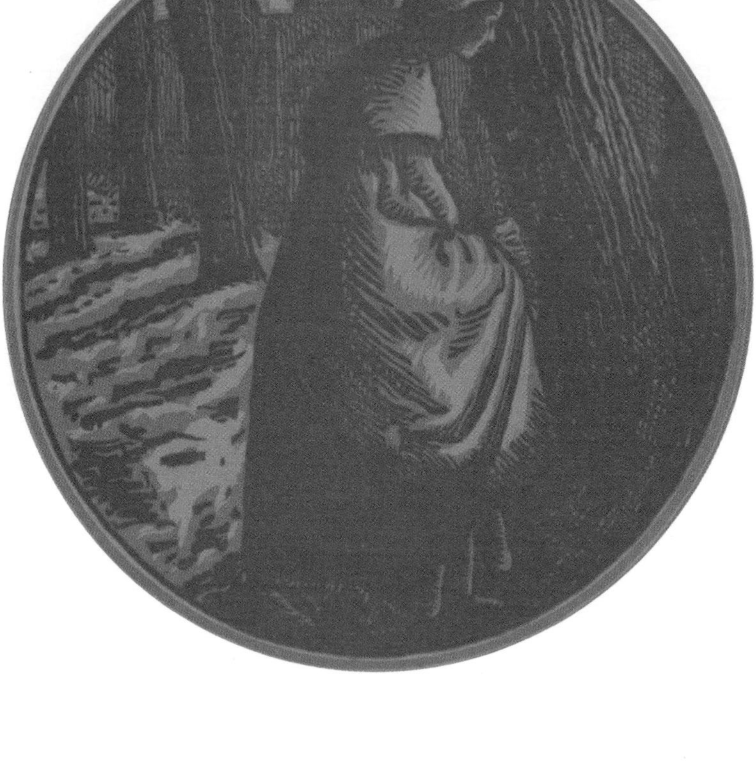

Above and opposite
Coleridge. *Christabel, Kubla Khan, Fancy in Nubibus, and Song from Zapolya*
1904

CHRISTABEL,
KUBLA KHAN,
FANCY IN NUBIBUS, & A SONG,
BY SAMUEL T. COLERIDGE.

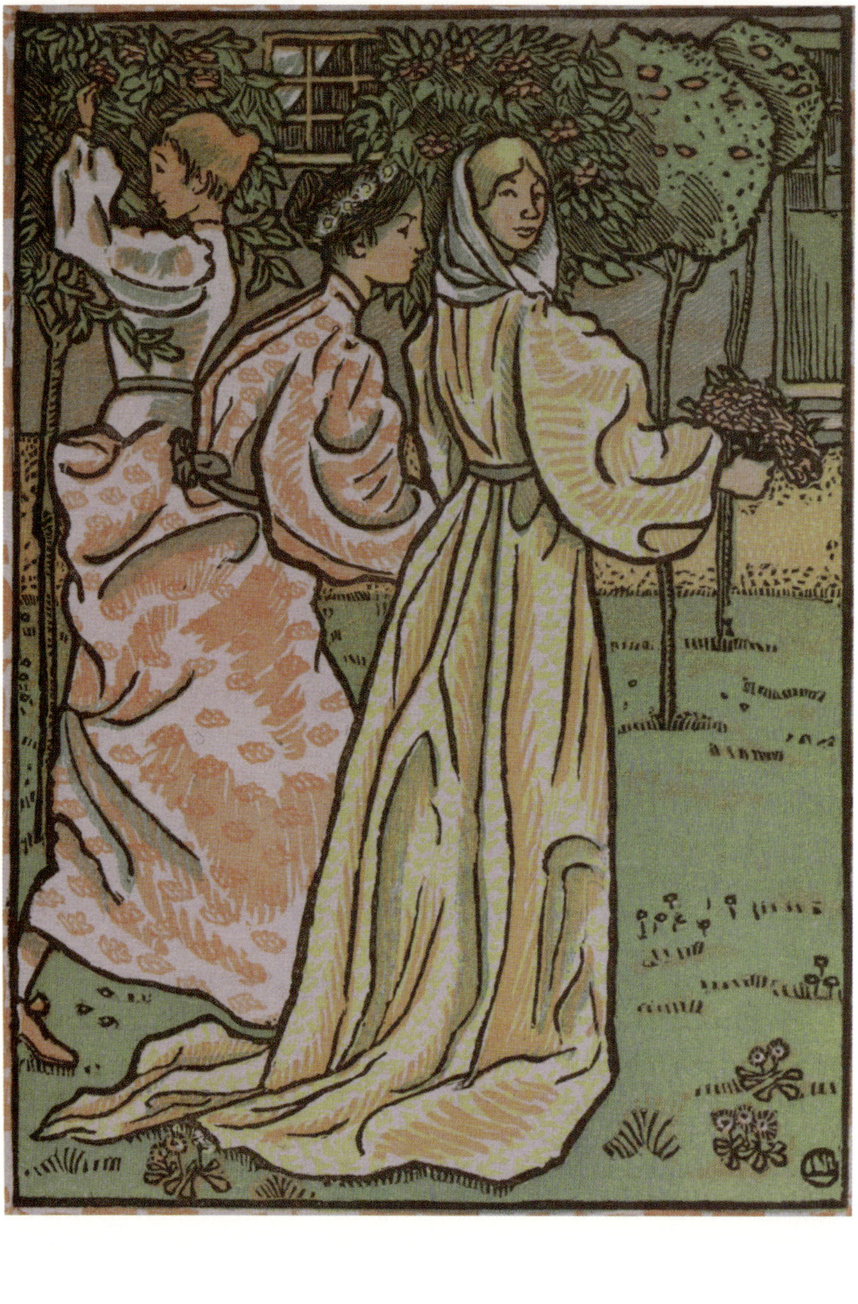

Browning
Some Poems by Robert Browning
1904

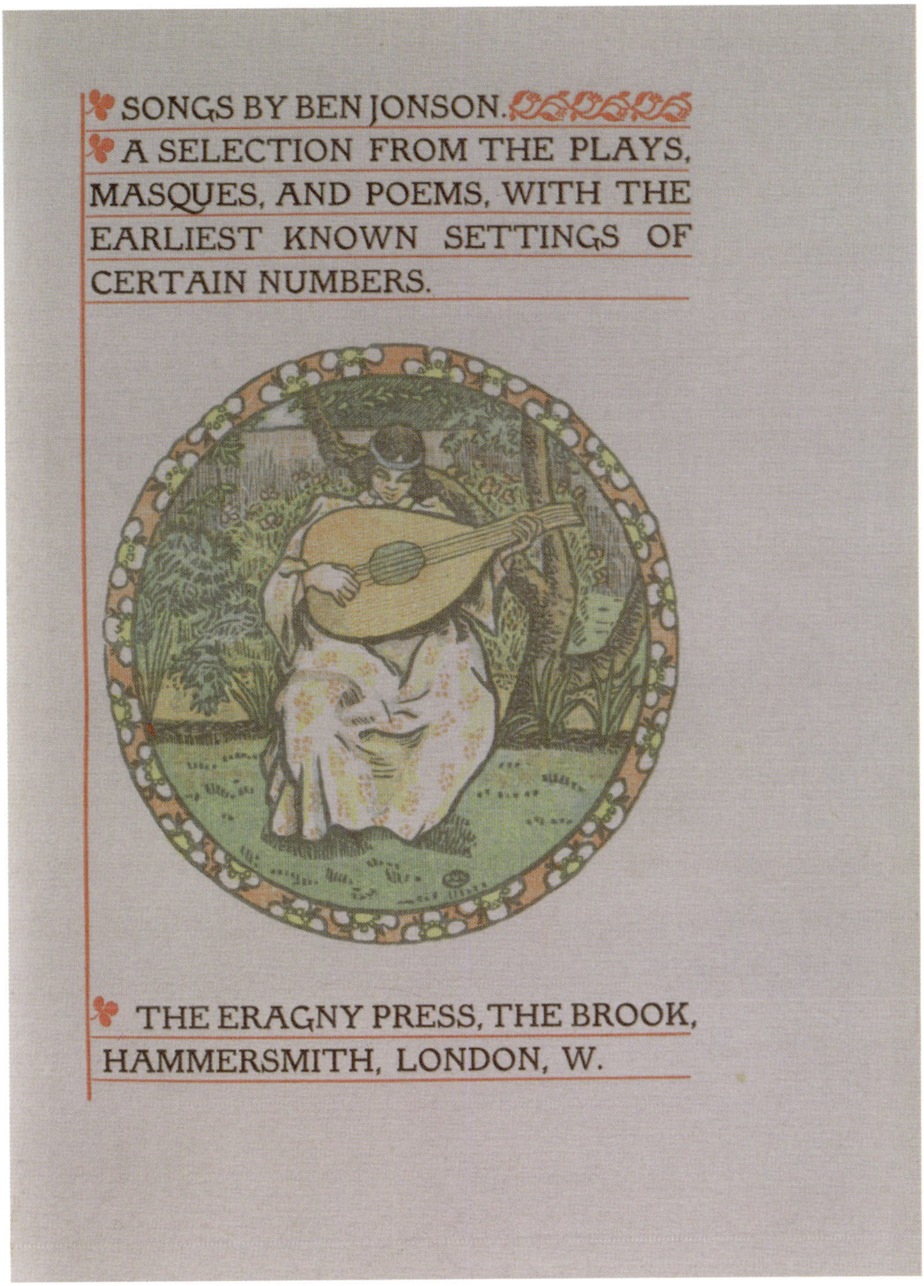
SONGS BY BEN JONSON.
A SELECTION FROM THE PLAYS, MASQUES, AND POEMS, WITH THE EARLIEST KNOWN SETTINGS OF CERTAIN NUMBERS.

THE ERAGNY PRESS, THE BROOK, HAMMERSMITH, LONDON, W.

Jonson
Songs by Ben Jonson
1906

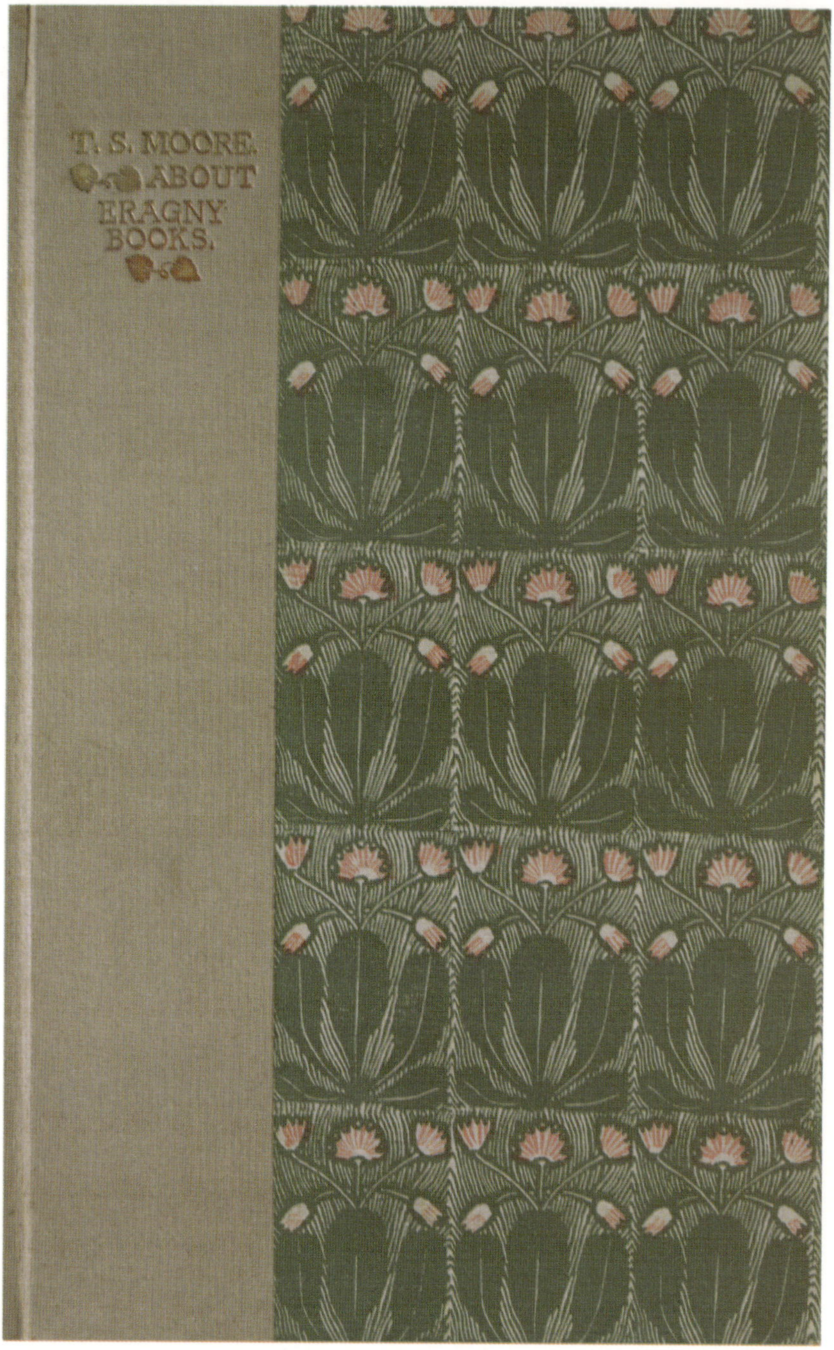

Moore
A Brief Account of the Origin of the Eragny Press
1903

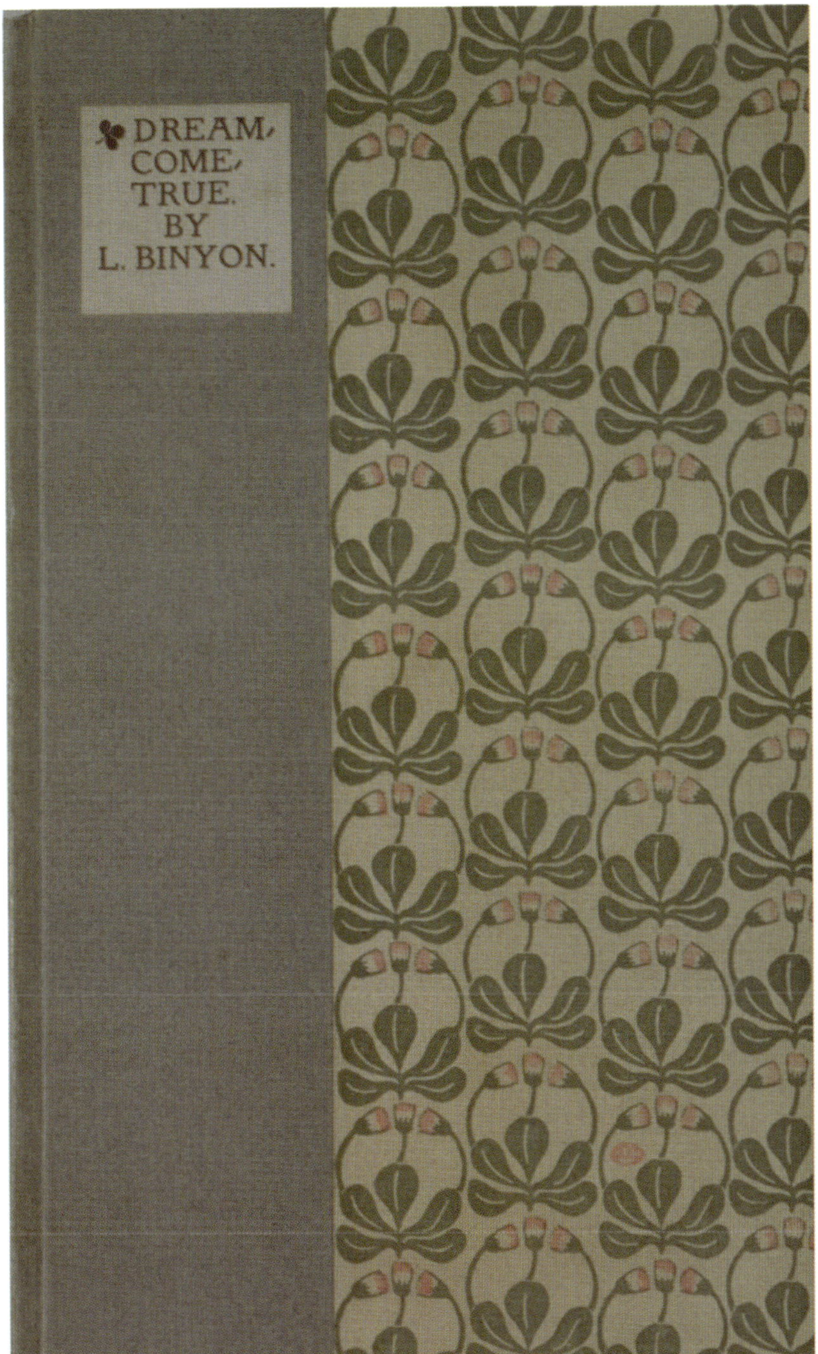

Binyon
Dream Come True
1905

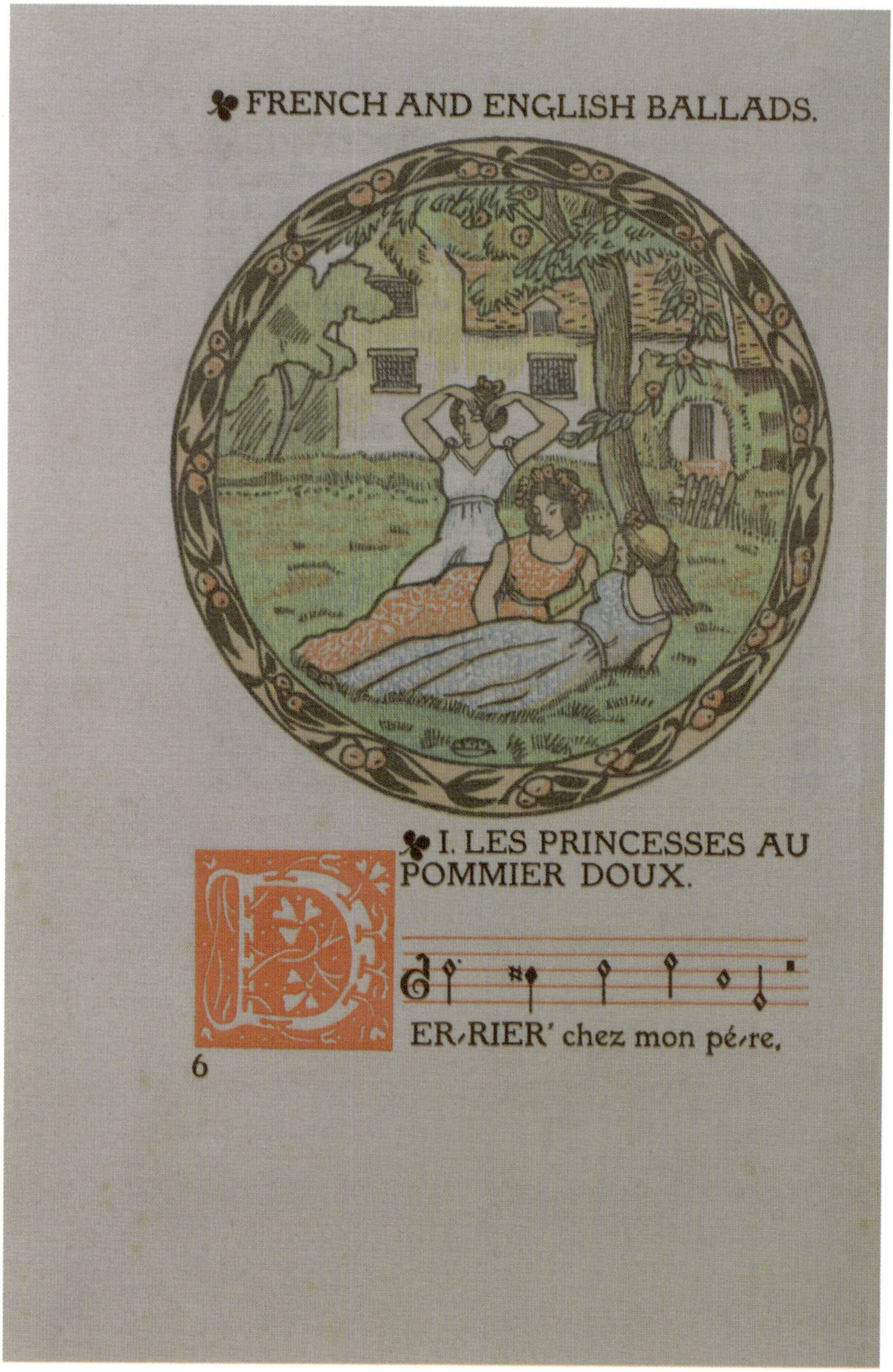

Steele
Some Old French and English Ballads
1905

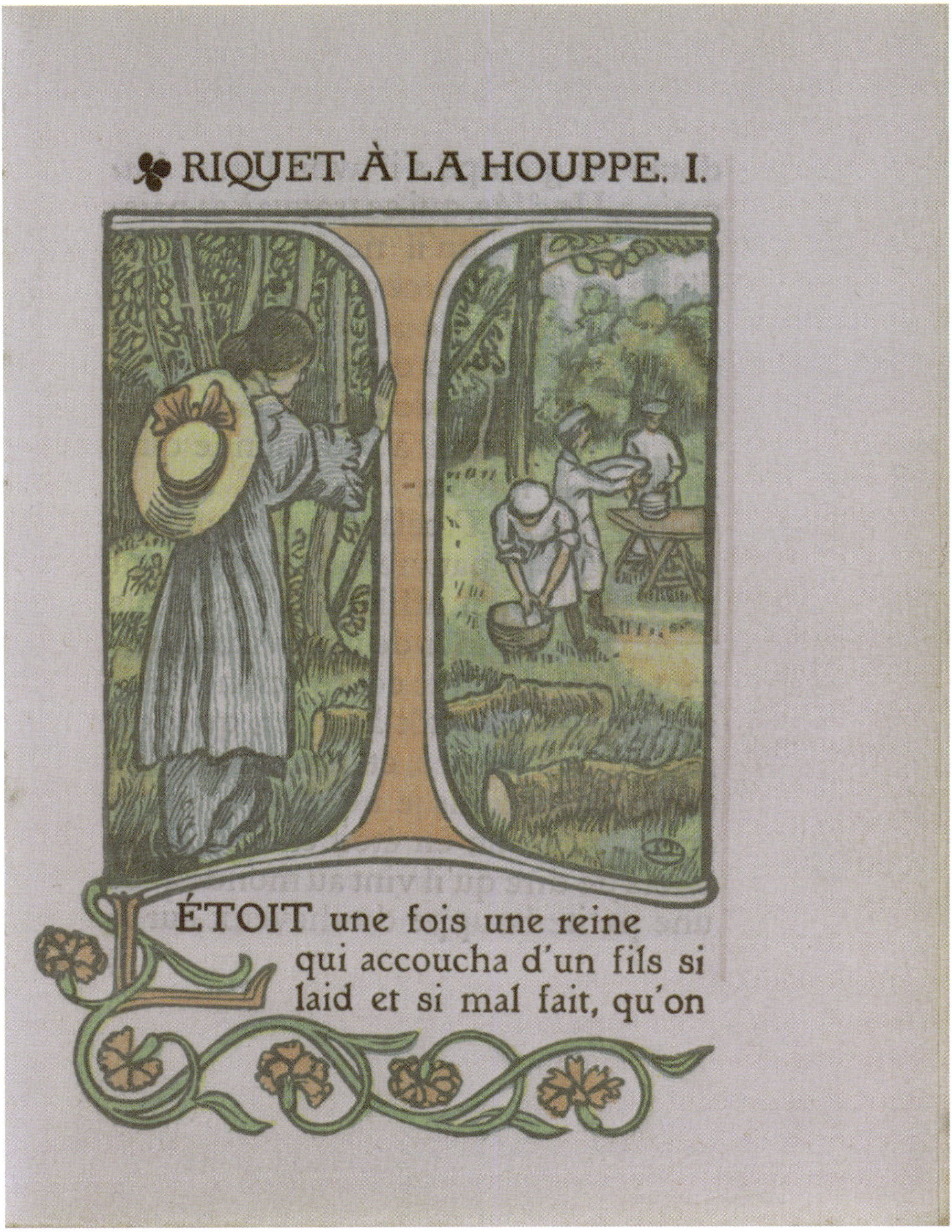
RIQUET À LA HOUPPE. I.

IL ÉTOIT une fois une reine qui accoucha d'un fils si laid et si mal fait, qu'on

Perrault
Riquet à la Houppe
1907

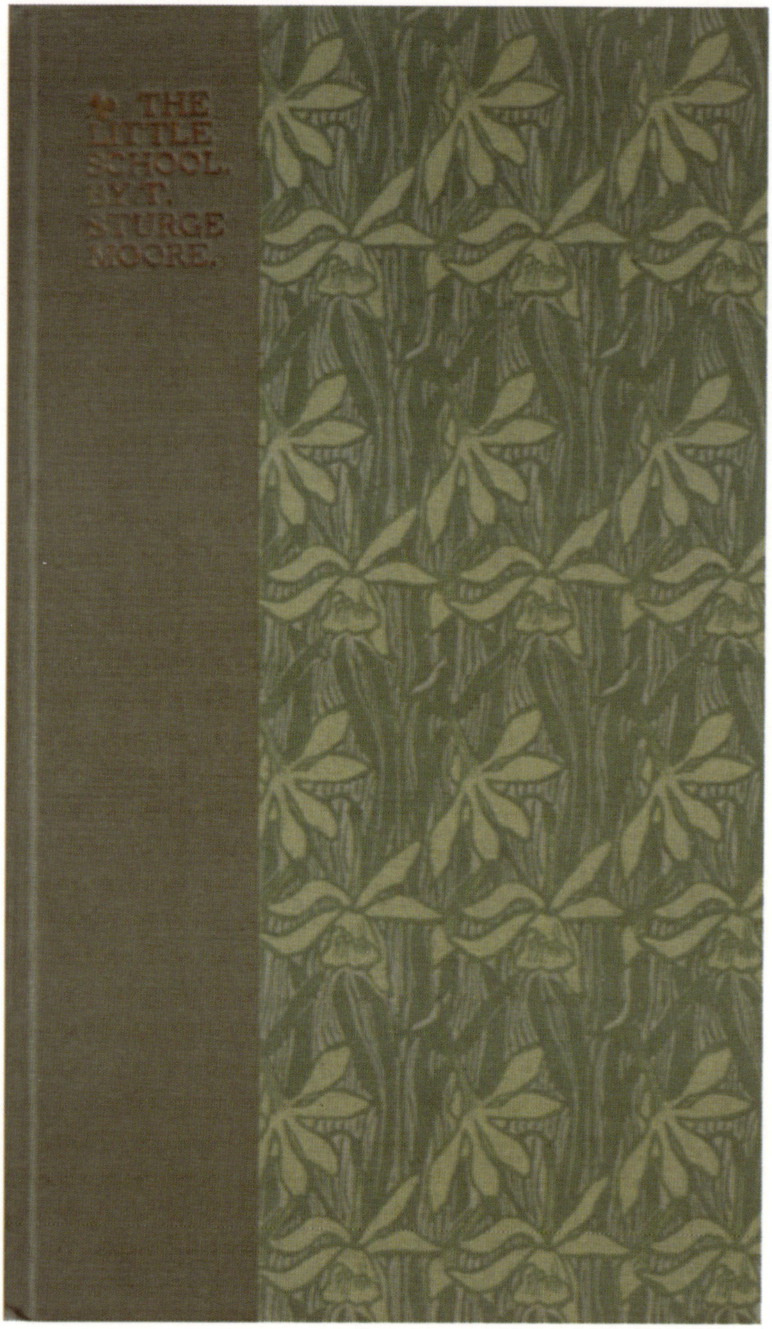

Moore
The Little School, a Posy of Rhymes
1905

Opposite
Nerval. *Histoire de la Reine du Matin et de Soliman Ben Daoud.* 1909

HISTOIRE DE LA REINE DU MATIN & DE SOLIMAN PRINCE DES GÉNIES.

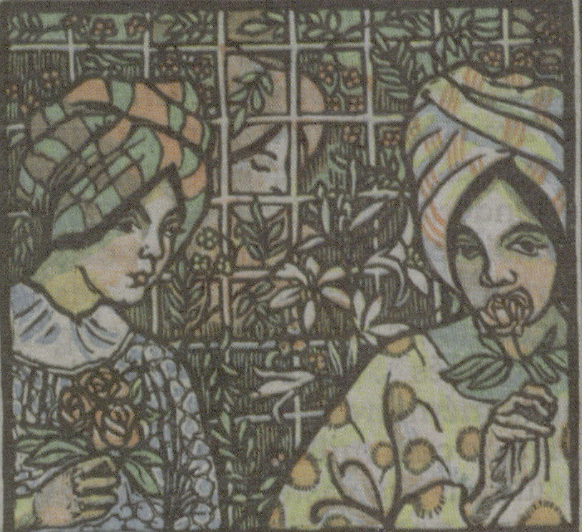

I. ADONIRAM.

POUR servir les desseins du grand roi Soliman Ben-Daoud, son serviteur Adoniram avait renoncé depuis

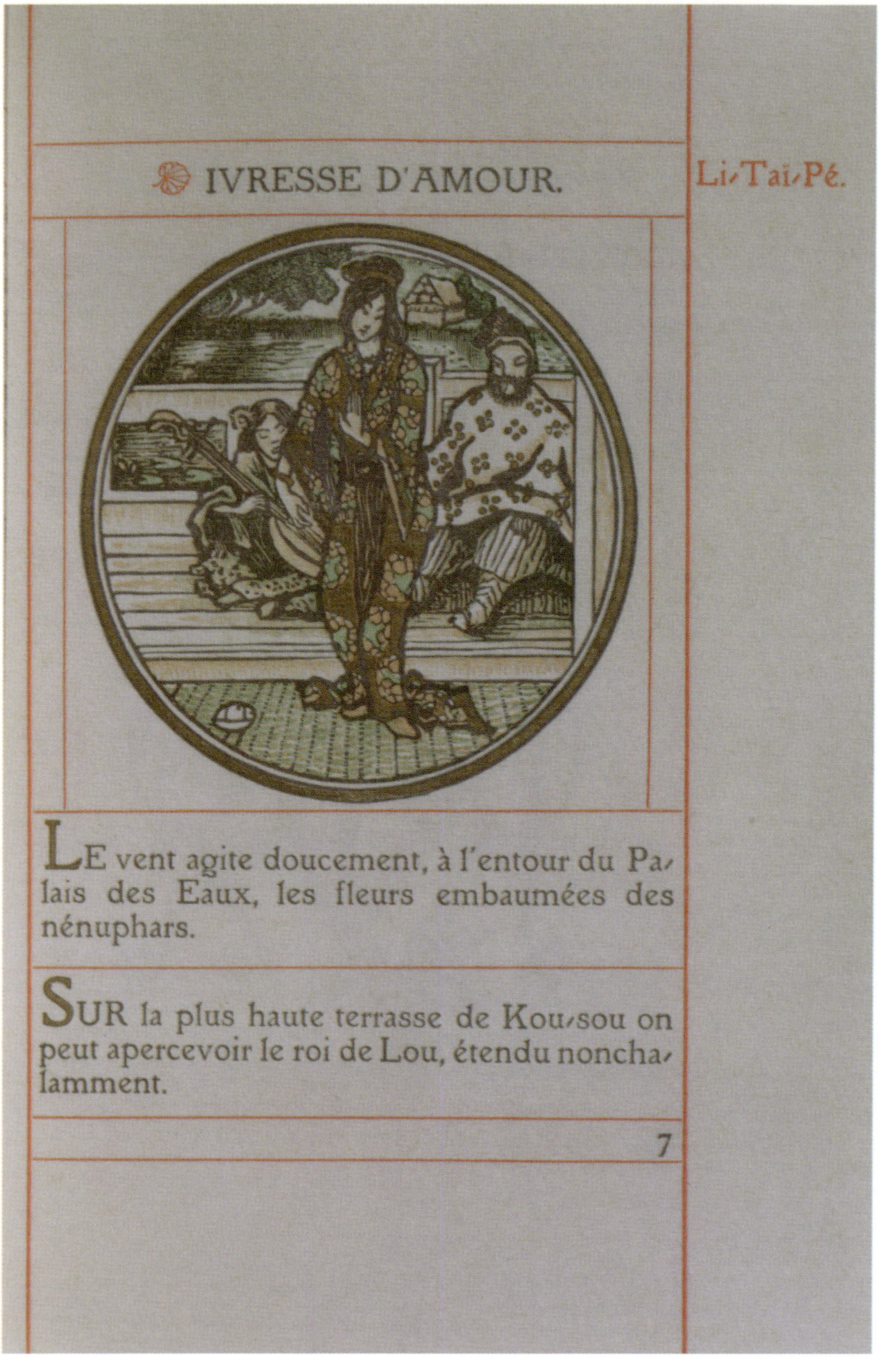

IVRESSE D'AMOUR.

Li-Taï-Pé.

LE vent agite doucement, à l'entour du Palais des Eaux, les fleurs embaumées des nénuphars.

SUR la plus haute terrasse de Kou-sou on peut apercevoir le roi de Lou, étendu nonchalamment.

7

Gautier
Poems Tirés du Livre de Jade, Ivresse d'Amour
1911

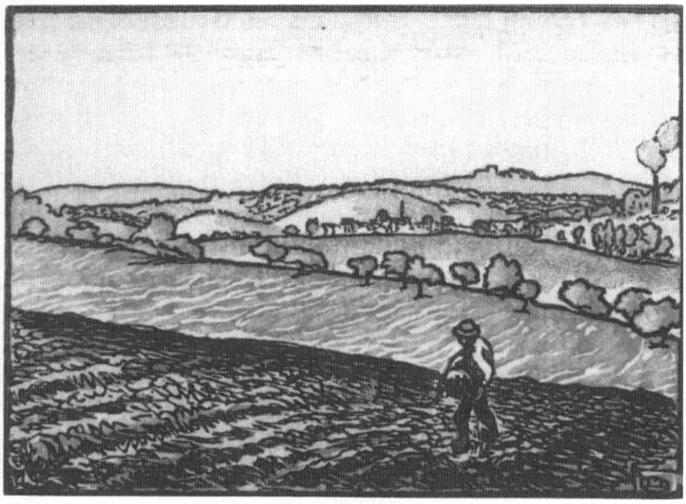

LES SEMAILLES.

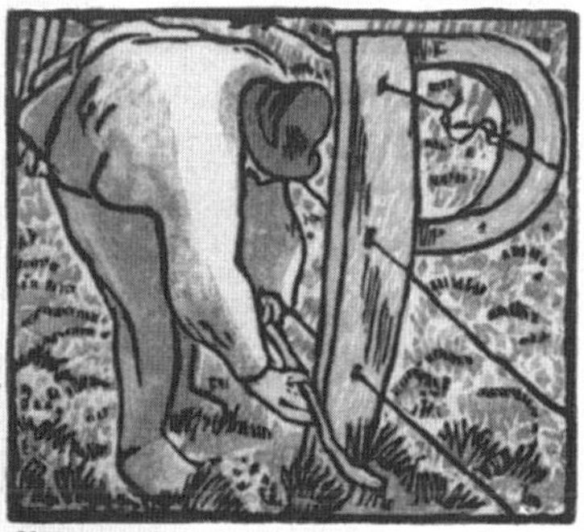

IERRE HERNEQUIN se tint, quelques instants, sur le seuil de sa maison, où tombait une averse tremblante de lumière.

Il avait enterré sa fem- me le matin même.

Le repas, qui suit ordi- nairement les funérail- les, venait de prendre fin, et la dernière carriole, reconduisant les parents dans les villages éloignés, disparaissait au loin, ta- che mouvante qui se rapetissait, se fondait dans l'immensité brune de cette terre de Beauce.

27

Figure xviii
Moselly
La Charrue d'Erable
1912

perfectly suited to Lucien's Franco-English sensibilities. Colin Franklin has argued that ". . . Brook type, on the white paper of the small pages in Eragny books, was the most beautiful fount invented in this whole period."[23] (Figure xx)

Despite the setbacks in 1903, the last eleven years of produc-

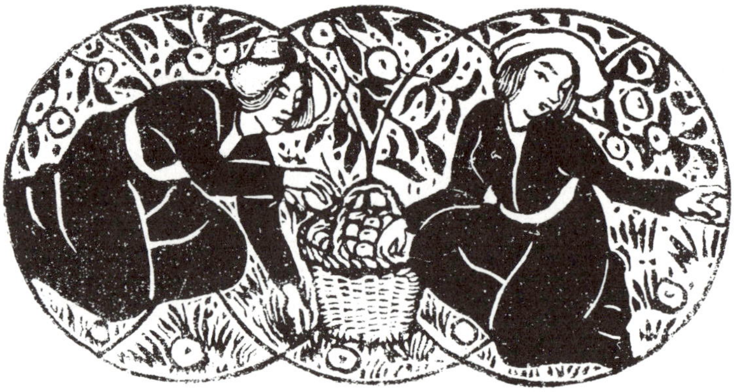

Figure xix
Nerval
Histoire de la Reine du Matin et de Soliman Ben Daoud
1909

tion saw the return of color to Eragny Press publications. In this work Lucien truly flourished. His renewed palette (opposing hues of red and green, yellow and purple) revealed his background in Neo-Impressionist color theory, but his distinctive accomplishment was due in part to subtle inking. (See color plates) Lucien almost never printed a color flat. Each block, cut to print a single color, was mottled to produce a pattern and inked with a delicate tint. The blocks of pale color were then carefully printed one over the next so that the viewer had to look closely to understand what was causing the spectral vibration. The colors were printed wet on wet, and the paper was kept damp so that the sheet did not shrink between color applications. Occasionally, Lucien even published an entire volume on colored papers. *Abrégé de l'Art Poetique Français* by Pierre de Ronsard, 1903, has been seen printed on a light pink sheet, on light green, and occasionally with tinted inks, in addition to the regular black and white edition. Unfortunately, the re-introduction of color meant an even larger outlay of time and money.

Opposite
Figure xx
Prospectus for Riquet à la Houppe *set in the Brook type*
1907

23. Franklin, *Private Presses*, 1969. p. 98.

THE ERAGNY PRESS, THE BROOK, HAMMERSMITH, LONDON, W.

(No. 12). NOW READY.

RIQUET À LA HOUPPE. (DEUX VERSIONS D'UN CONTE DE MA MÈRE LOYE).

NOTICE: The first of these two versions is by Charles Perrault; the second is from a XVIIth. Century manuscript in the Mazarine Library in Paris. It is by an unknown writer, who at the same time as Perrault, had the idea of collecting French folk tales. His version is very different from Perrault's celebrated tale, and is nearer the legend of the gnome Ruebezahl as Musaeus gathered it from the peasants of the Hartz mountains.

With two original woodcuts designed & engraved by L. Pissarro, in which large decorative initials frame small illustrations. These are printed in four colours.

Bound with blue Michallet paper sides, vellum back and coloured label.

Small Demy 16mo.

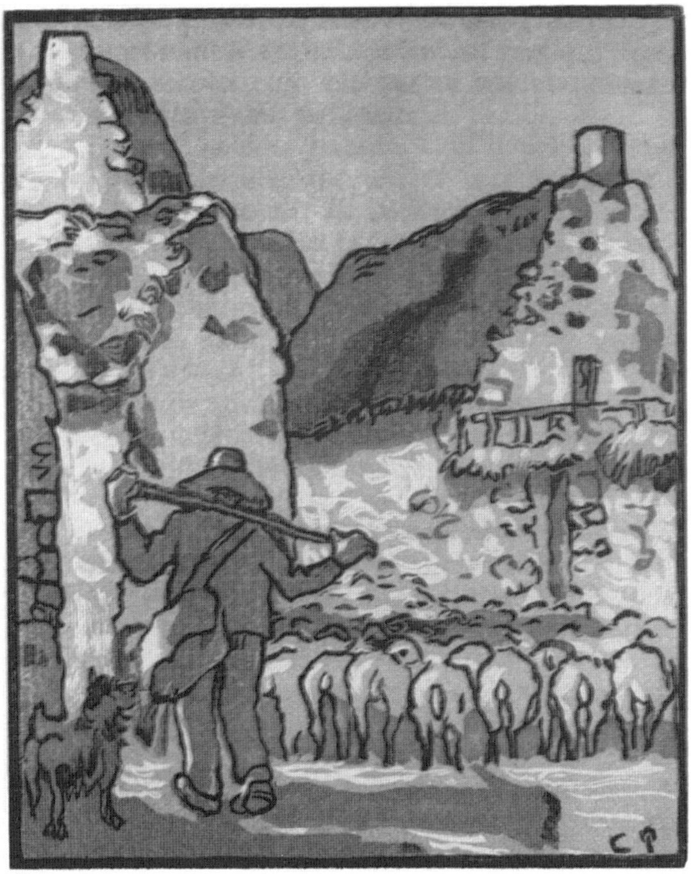

Figure xxi
Moselly
La Charrue d'Erable
1912

By 1905 Lucien and Esther had begun to reduce the size of their editions and the number of books produced in order to lower their costs. Whereas in 1903, at the height of their output, they published five titles in editions of around 240, in 1905 and again in 1906, they published only three, in editions of 200 or

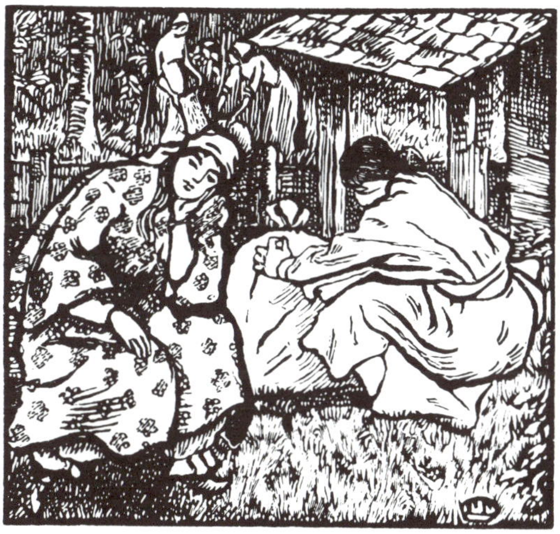

Figure xxii
Nerval
Histoire de la Reine du Matin et de Soliman Ben Daoud
1909

less. The following seven years, between 1907 and 1914 when the press closed, production dropped significantly and only a total of five books were produced in editions no larger than 130. Moreover, two of those books were wholly subsidized by publishing commissions.

In 1909 and again in 1912 the Eragny Press received the prestigious honor of requisitions to produce books from two French bibliophile clubs. Each should have been a profit-making venture, but once again, due to highly technical production and Lucien's miscalculations of his expenses, any gains they might have made were wiped out. Gérard de Nerval's *Histoire de la Reine du Matin et de Soliman Ben Daoud* was commissioned by the Société des Cent Bibliophiles in 1909. The luxury of working with advanced capital and high quality materials enabled Lucien to construct a lavish book. Printed in colors and with gold leaf, it was excruciatingly detailed and took twenty months to produce.[24] The final composition included more than fifteen illustrations, seven border designs, and eleven historiated capitals. The leather-bound cover was patterned with gold-stamped flowers. (Figures xvii, xix, xxii, and color plates)

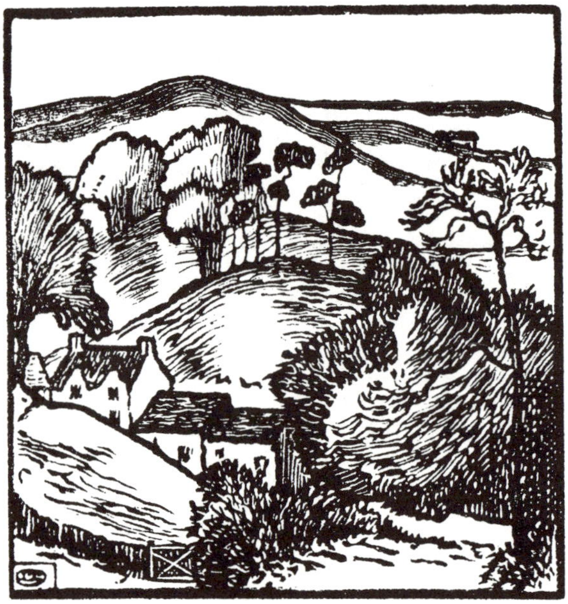

Figure xxiii
Landscape: Blackpool Devon
1914

Even more elaborate, though less ornate, was the book contracted for *Le Livre Contemporain* in 1911, *La Charrue de'Erable.* Finally, Lucien was able to interest a publisher in what had been his dream of a major collaboration between himself and his father. Ironically, the work may have been even better for the wait: After long negotiations with the publisher, not only did Lucien agree to produce the twelve woodcuts after his father's drawings, but he filled out the volume with many of his own creations. Each of Camille's twelve drawings, reproduced in the close tonalities of the chiaroscuro method, had a small chapter

24. Genz, p. 189 *passim*. Lucien proudly used gold leaf in his work, not powder. The gold was always applied first so as not to stick to the wet ink of the other colors being used. First, the block was inked with a varnish and that varnish was printed on the damp paper. A gold sheet was then adhered carefully to the paper and hopefully stuck only to the varnished sections.

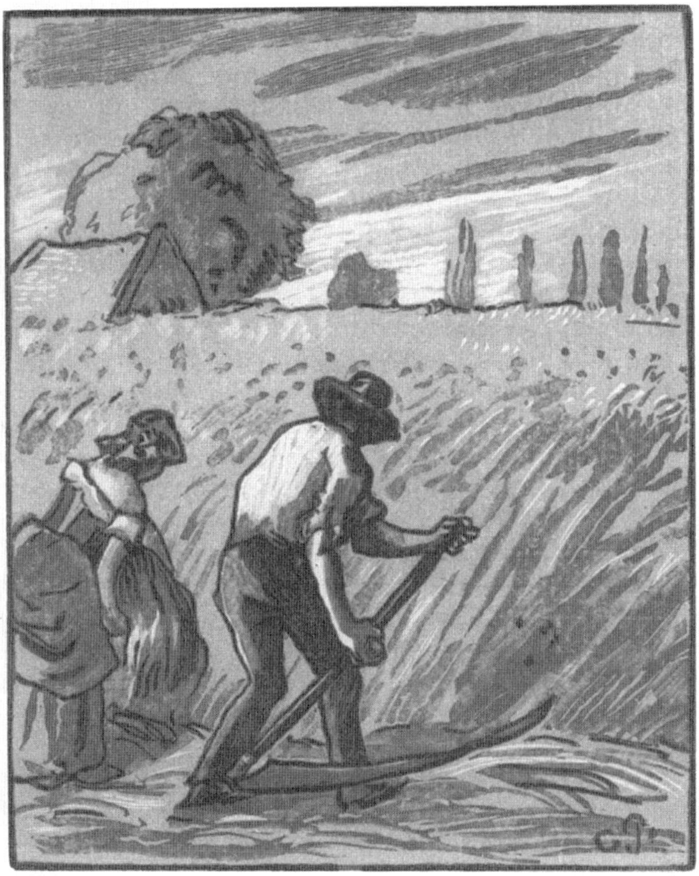

Figure xxiv
Moselly
La Charrue d'Erable
1912

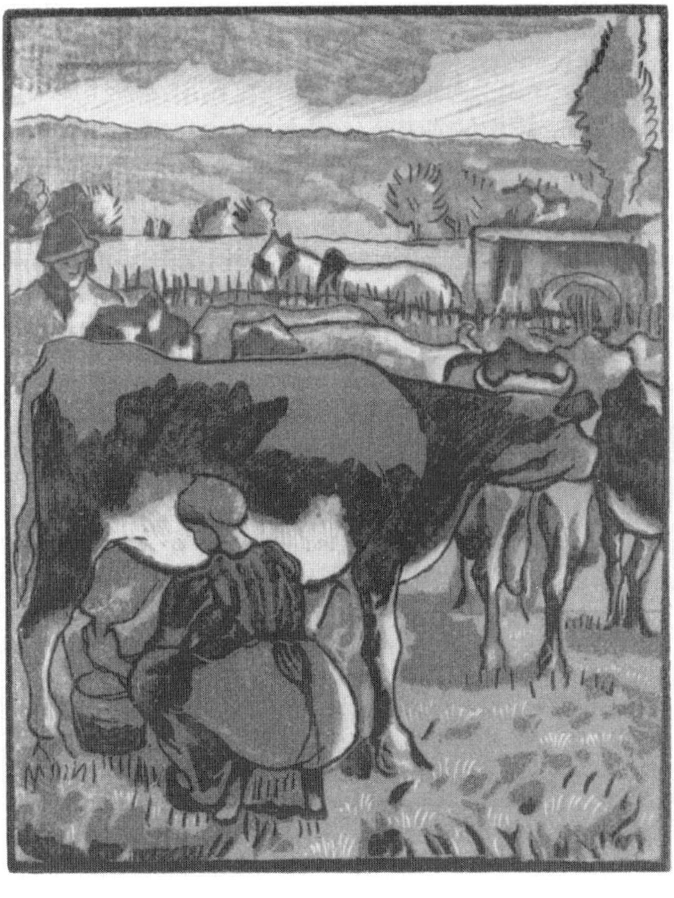

Figure xxv
Moselly
La Charrue d'Erable
1912

written around it by the writer Emile Moselly. Lucien then embellished the text with illustrated head and tail pieces and historiated capitals. The edition took more than two years to assemble and most of Lucien's profit was spent in production. (Figures xxi, xxiv, and xxv)

When World War I broke out, the Eragny Press was forced to close. Lucien and Esther were no longer able to import their specially handmade paper from France, but more importantly, the War caused them to lose touch with their regular collectors not only on the continent, but worldwide.[25] Neither partner anticipated more than just a temporary halt to production, but when the war was over, they found themselves without the capital to begin again. Lucien, who had already returned to painting before the close of the Press, continued to paint and exhibit his work until the end of his life in 1944.

In its twenty years of operation the Eragny Press produced thirty-two titles. Included in those books were more than 300 wood-engraved illustrations, borders and fancy capitals representing about seventy percent of Lucien's entire printed oeuvre.[26] Unlike Kelmscott and Vale before it, and the many other private presses that began in the 1890s, the Eragny Press was not a lucrative business operation. The small format books were not highly priced yet were very labor intensive. Nor did they resemble their competitors in character. Eragny books, with their beautiful flowered covers, were unique in their skillful combination of French and English aesthetics. It was an unlikely synthesis of English Arts and Crafts design and French impressionistic interest in color, light and sensations after nature. Ironically, this same charming quality may have made the work less marketable. Although Lucien chose his titles to appeal to a cross section of interests, to the English the books may have seemed too French,

25. There were several serious collectors of Eragny Press books in the United States, including J.M. Andreini, H. Alfred Fowler and John Quinn.

26. Lucien also made several lithographs and approximately thirty-four etchings.

and to the French the books were a bit too English. Moreover, the volumes produced during the Vale association were printed in French to attract the continental collectors, but their aesthetic quality at that time was at its most Pre-Raphaelite. The second half of the Eragny output was almost all printed in English, yet they were perhaps the most "French" in character.

Ultimately, what made Eragny Press books extraordinary — their complex production methods combined with simple artistic integrity — resulted in small output, little-to-no profit, and eventually led to the demise of the Press. In 1947, three years after Lucien's death, Esther, with the help of her nephew, cast the punches and matrices of the Brook type into the English Channel. It was a symbolic gesture to the two countries whose influence had mingled so beautifully in Lucien's work and whose national characters had helped to define the output of this small, but important, private press.

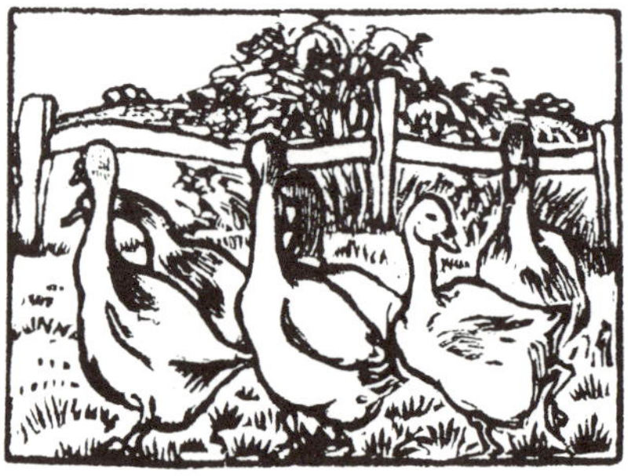

Figure xxvi
Geese
1903

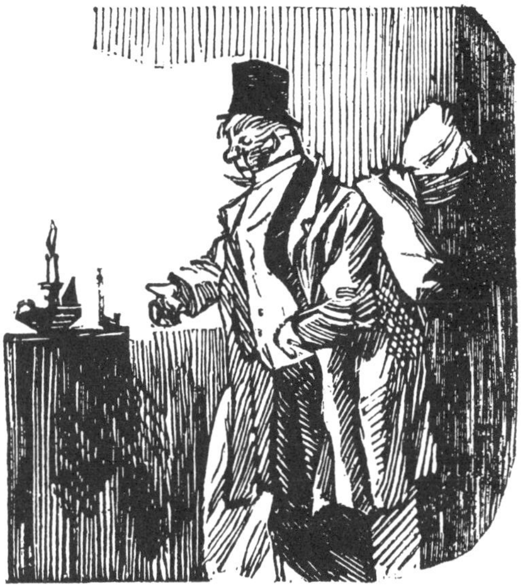

I
Copie de Ch. Keene
c. 1885

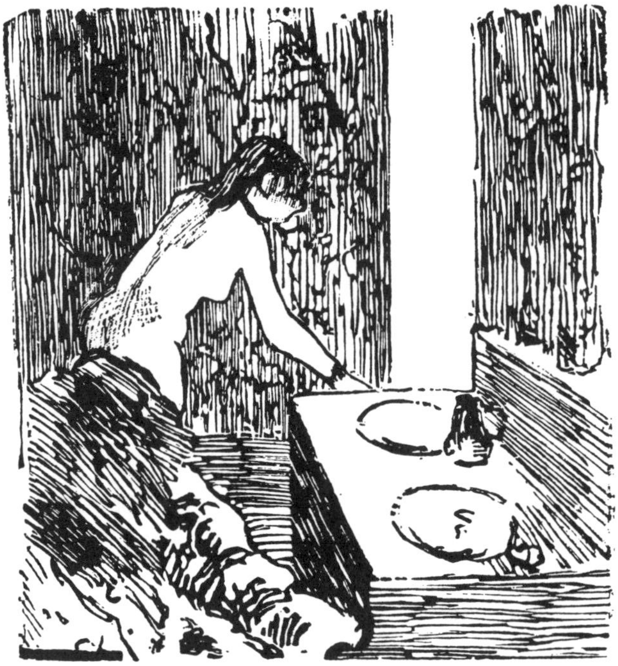

2
The Bath, after Degas
c. 1886

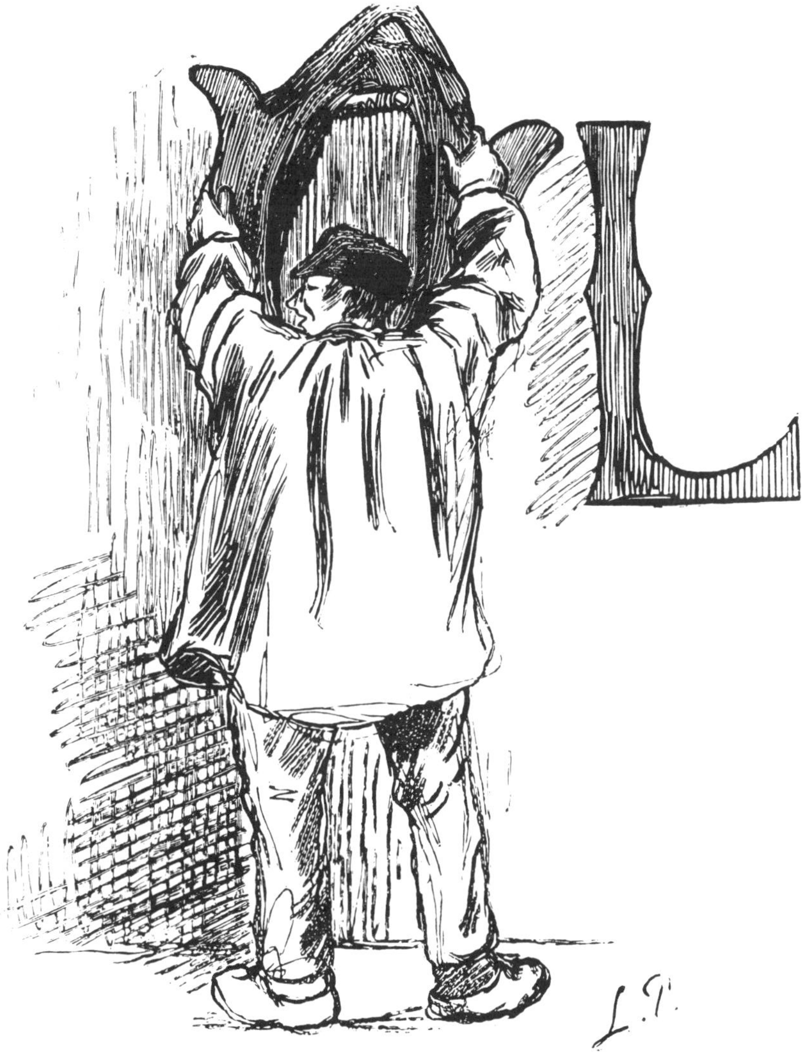

3
Mirbeau
Les Infortunes de Mait' Liziard, reduced
1886

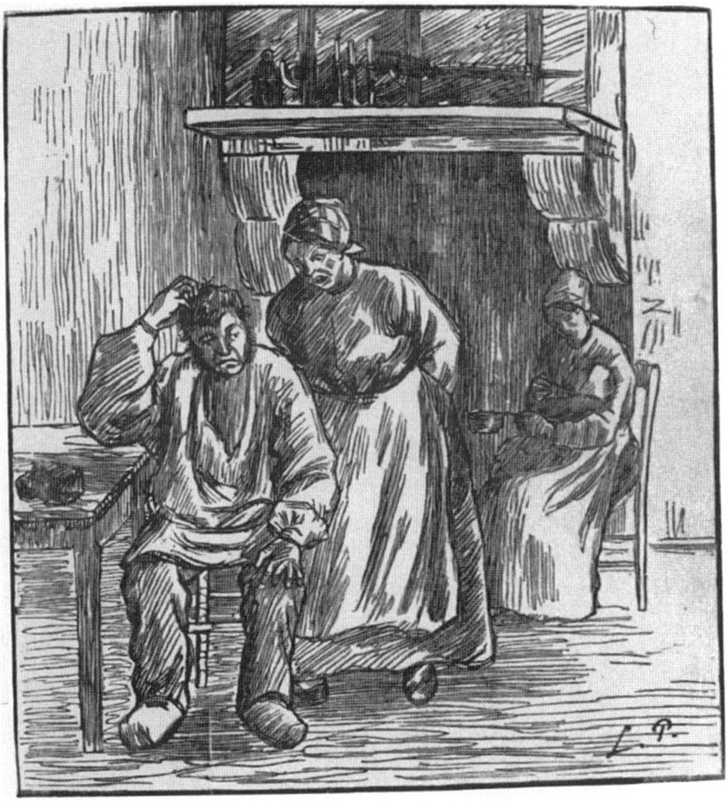

4
Mirbeau
Les Infortunes de Mait' Liziard
1886

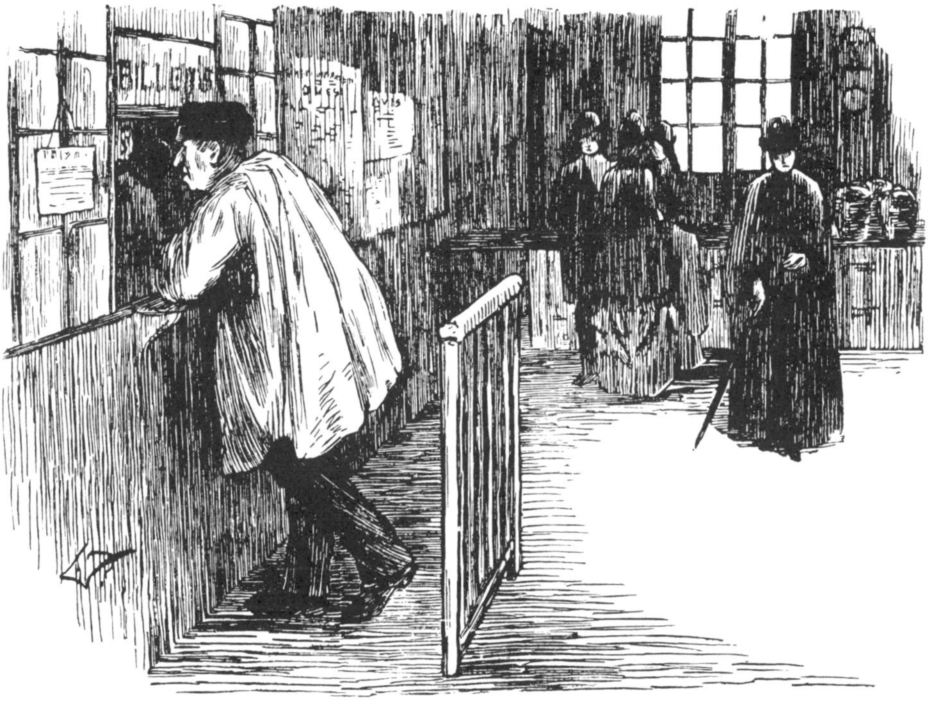

5
La Gare, reduced
1886

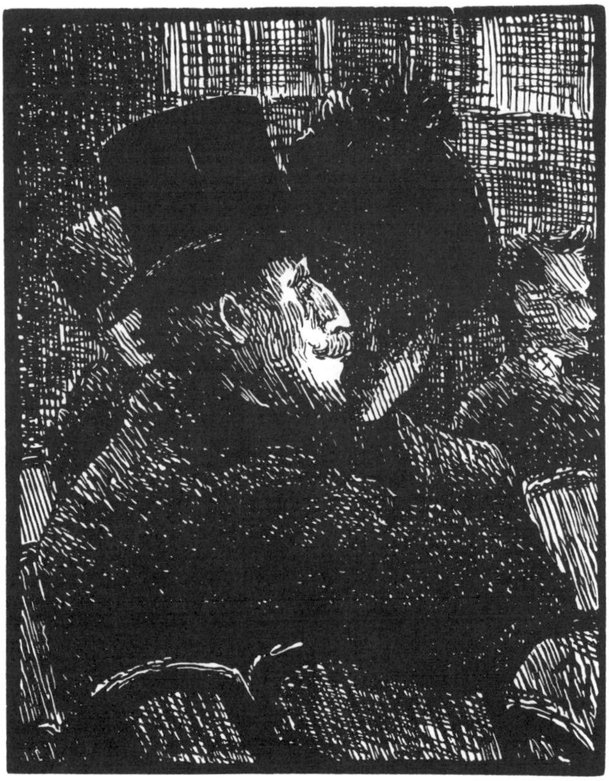

6
Au Café-Concert
c. 1888

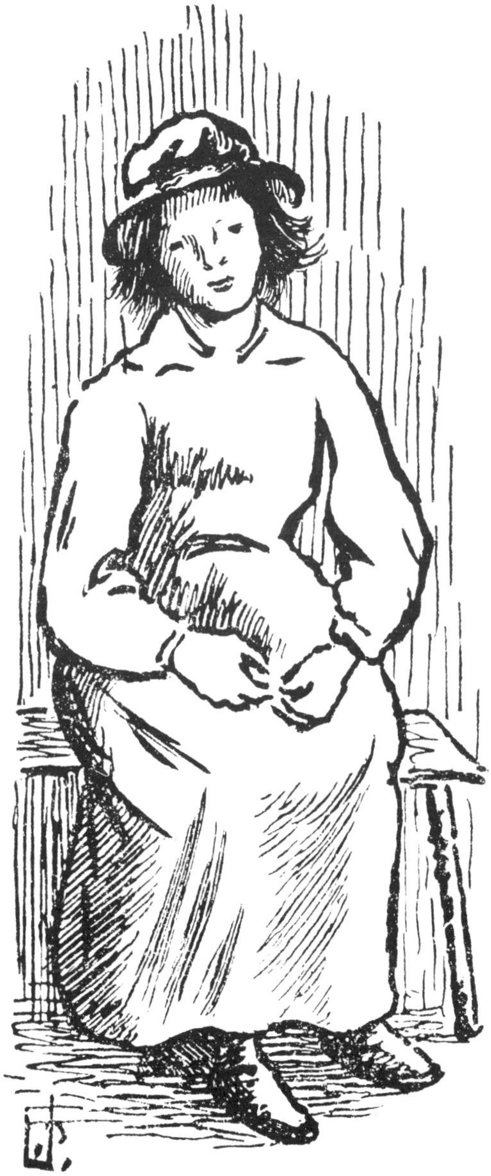

7
Jeune Fille
c. 1889

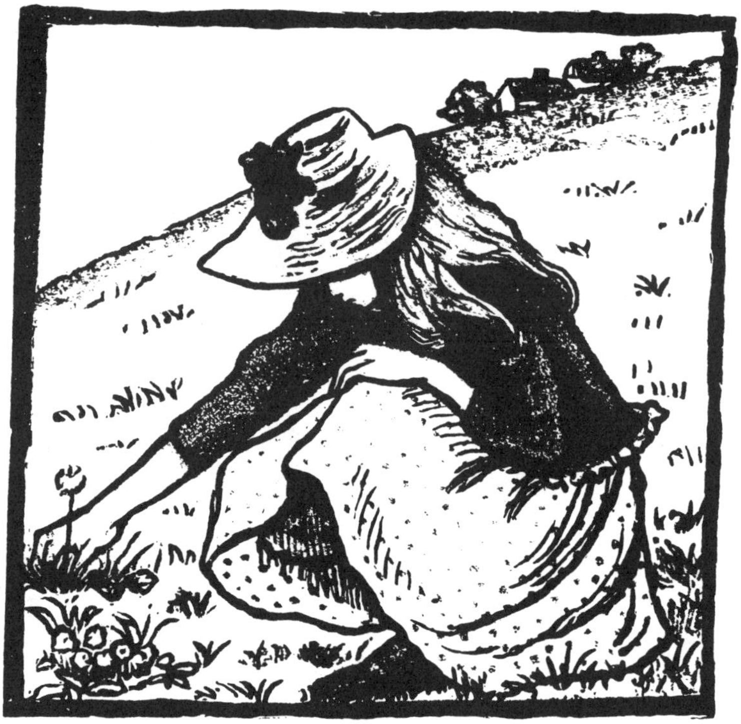

8
Little May
c. 1890

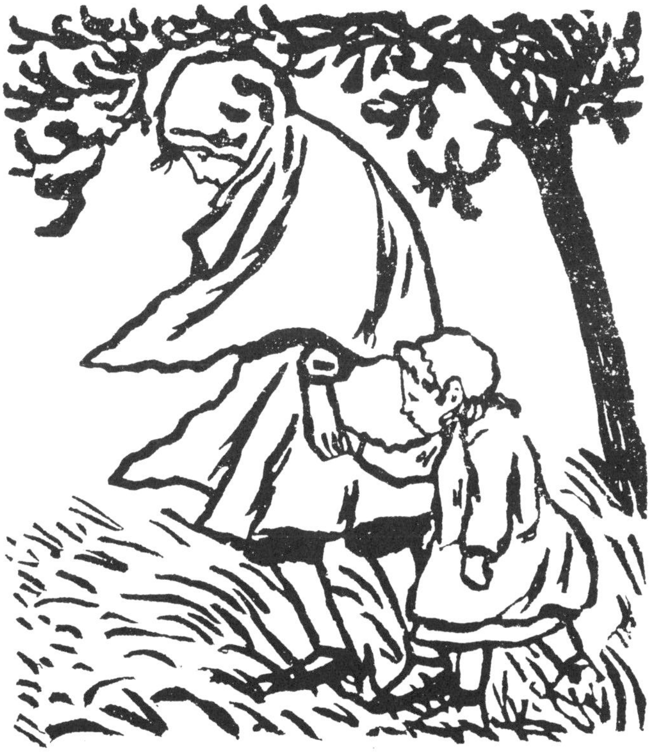

9
April
c. 1890

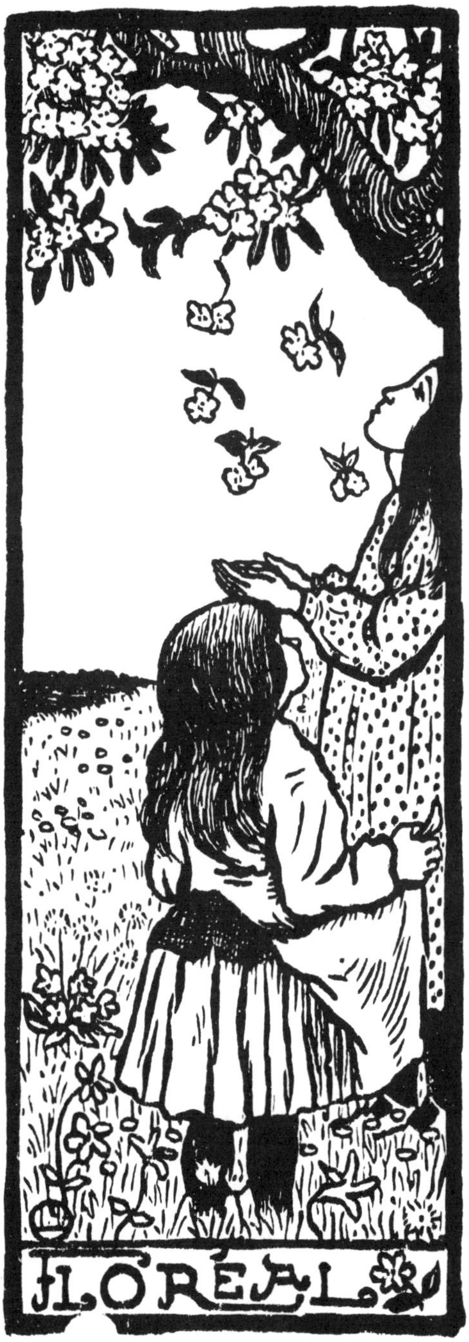

10
Floreal
1890

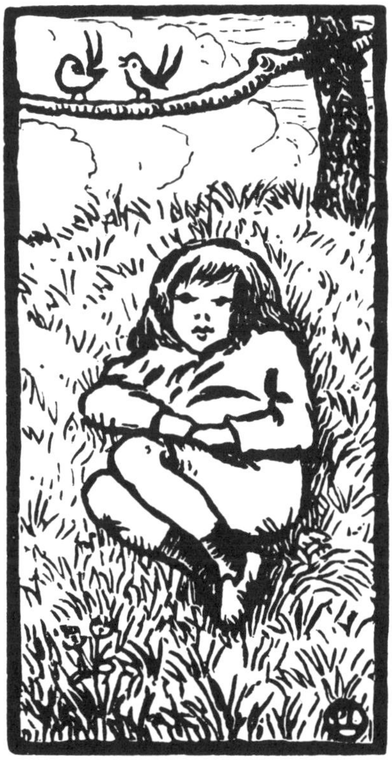

11
Contentment
1890

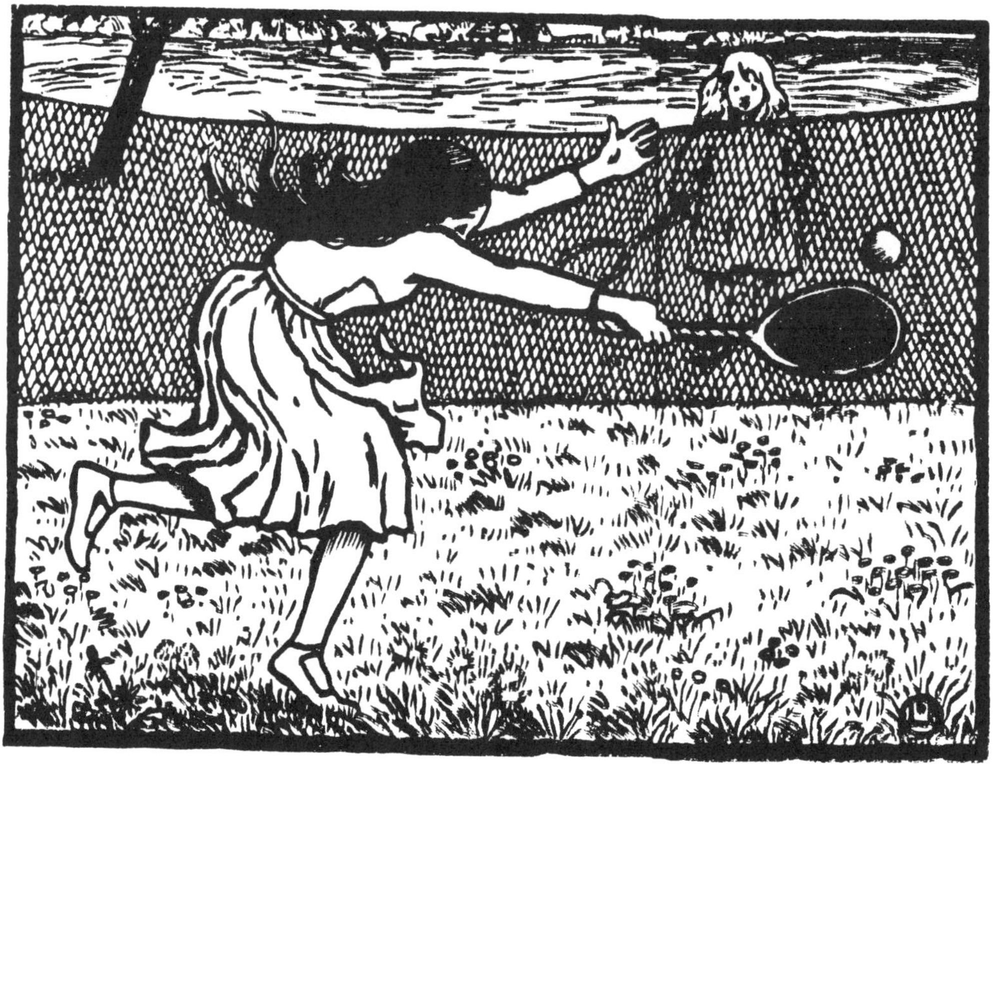

12
Le Tennis
1890

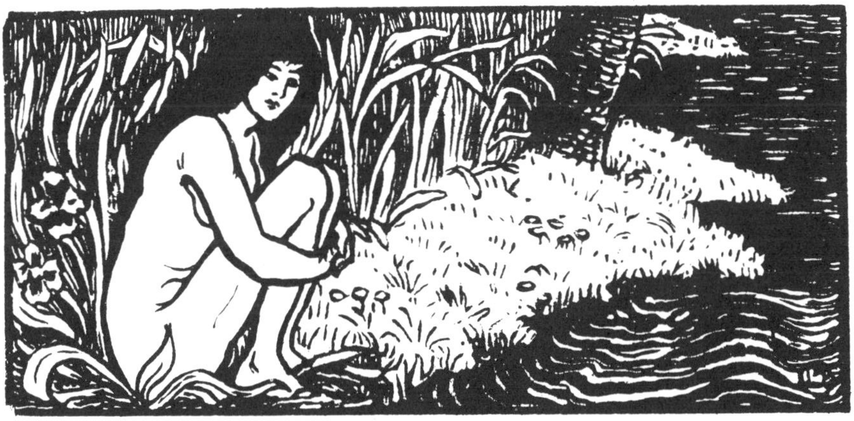

13
Baigneuse
1890

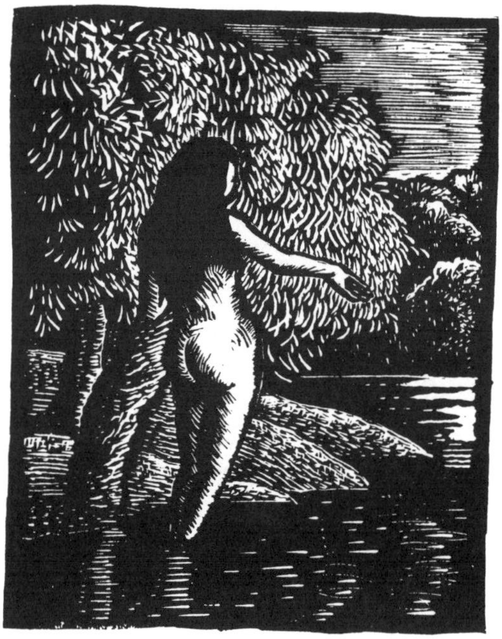

14
Femme au bois
c. 1891

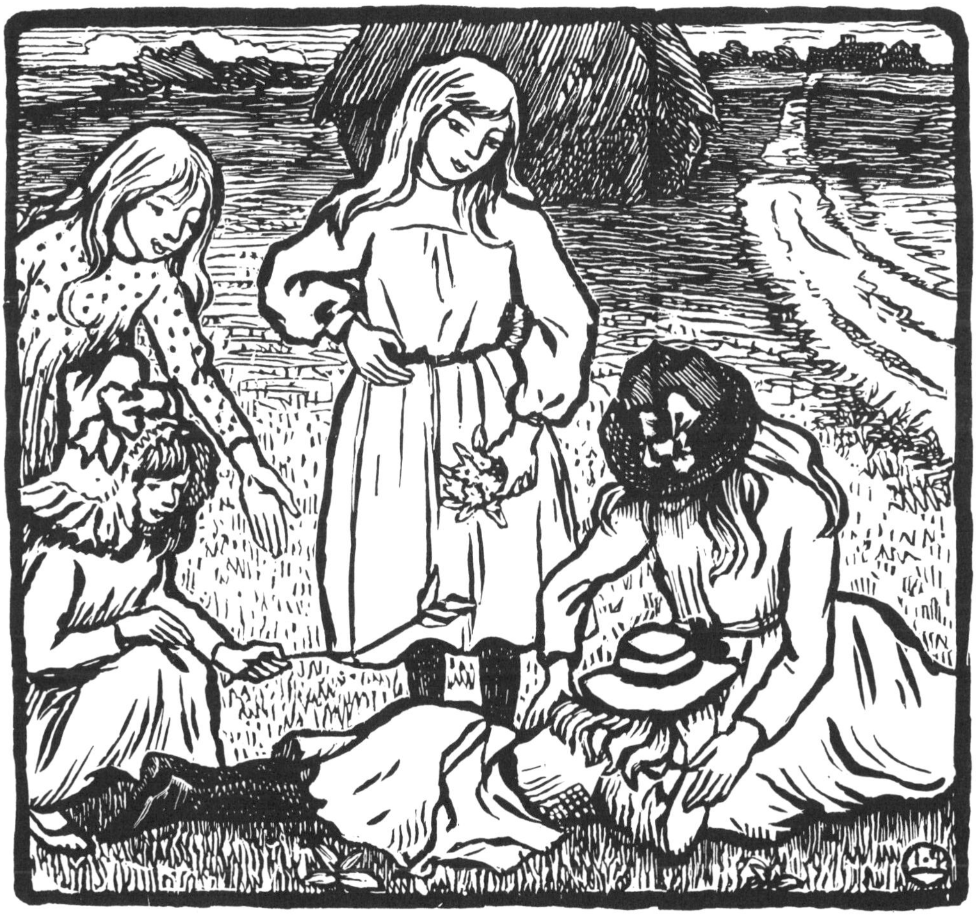

15
Enfants jouant
c. 1891

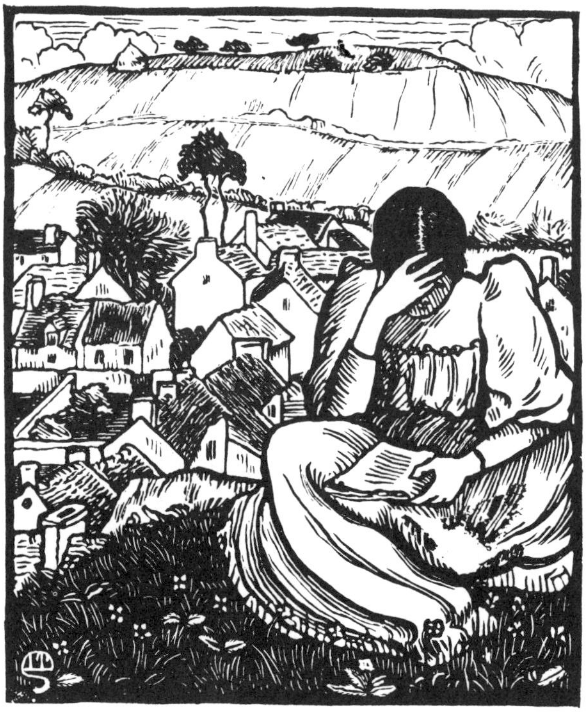

16
Liseuse
c. 1891

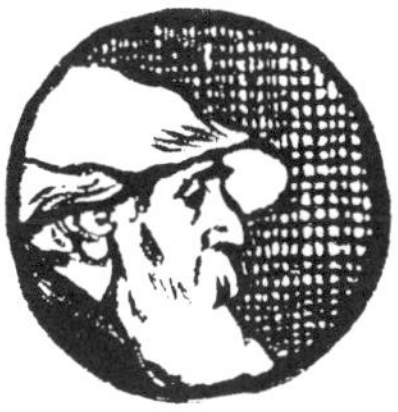

17
Portrait de Camille Pissarro
1892

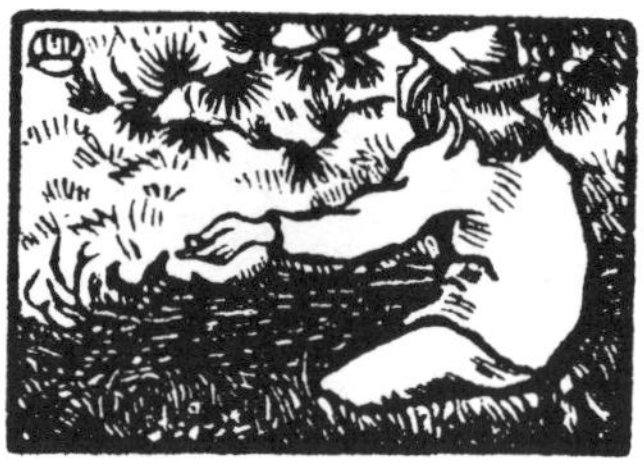

18
Boy and Pine Tree
1894

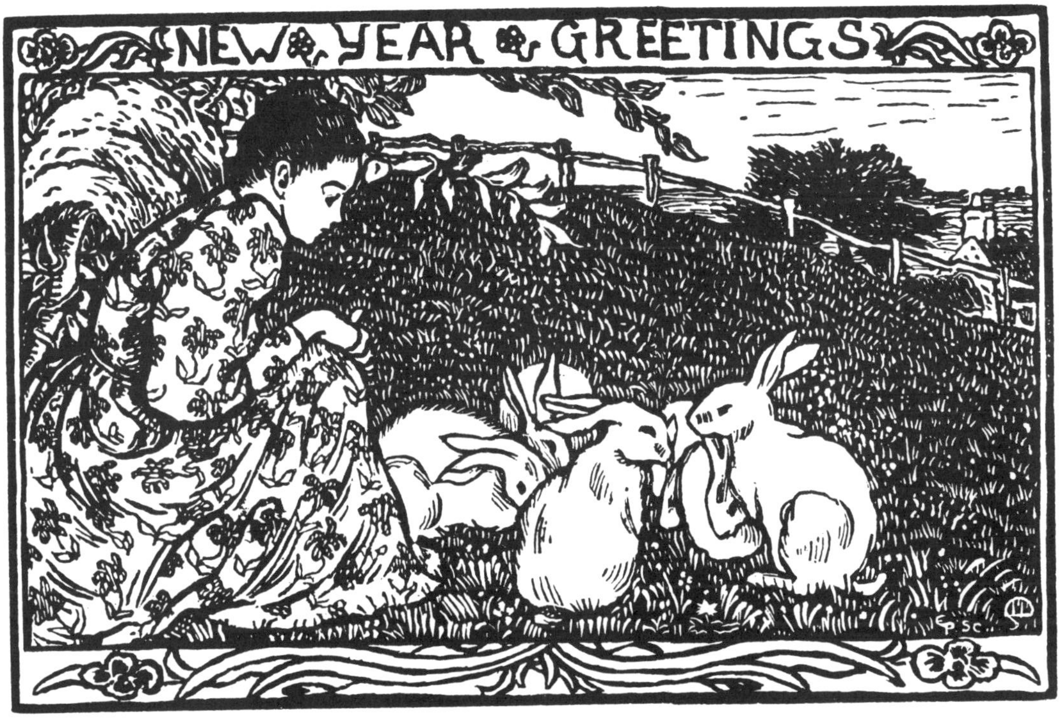

19
New Year Card
1893

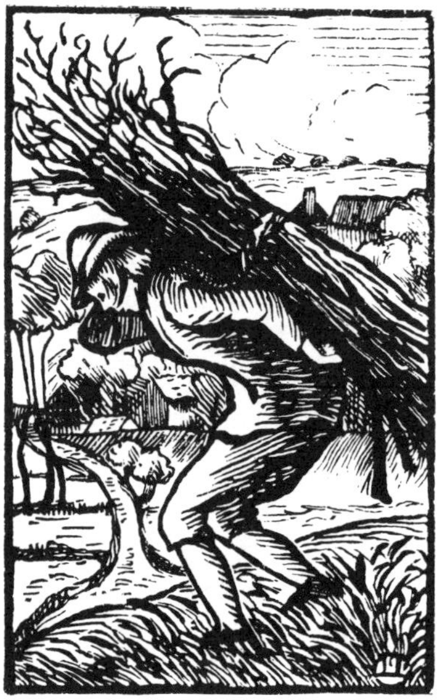

20
Rust
The Queen of the Fishes
1894

The Queen of the Fishes.

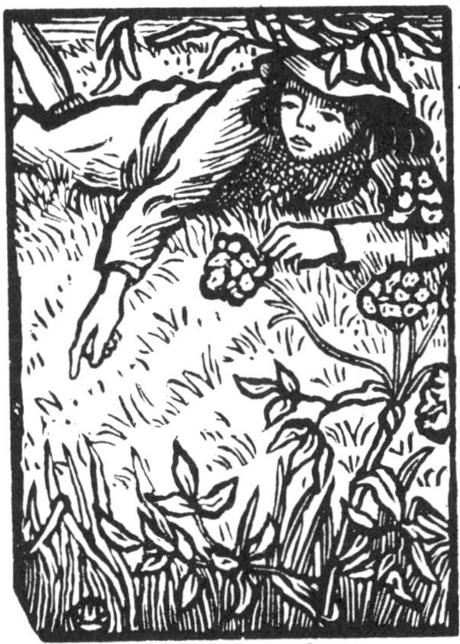

branches pointing up, gold-tipped, to the sky & out to the blue circle where the world ends. And looking down as he stood at the water's edge, he saw in the depths all the fishes of the river, the roach minnows & fierce old pike & all the great & little eels swimming & wriggling along in grand procession following a beautiful fish, her sides gleaming with scales of red red gold. As was his habit in the dream he cried "Ah, the QUEEN of the FISHES!" And he awoke. He sat up rubbing his eyes, & saw that it was evening & that the fairies

2

21
Rust
The Queen of the Fishes
1894

The Queen of the Fishes.

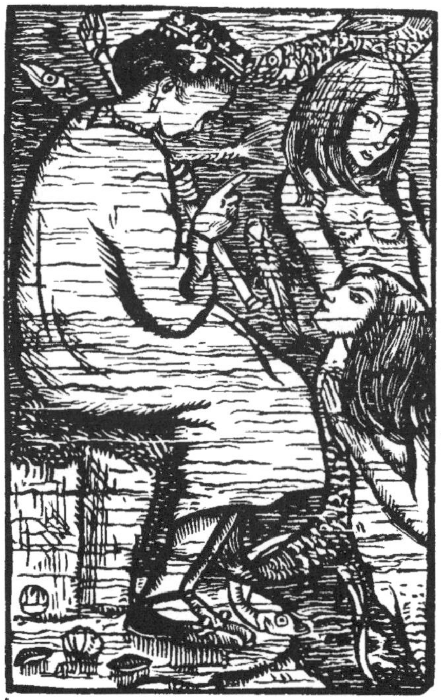

which seemed to them now only dreams. They had heard them often before yet he never tired of the story of her journeys under the clear water & the strange creatures & mermaids of her court where she was queen & how all the fishes swam about & played hide & seek with her in & out the water weeds. The boy seemed great & grand to the little fisher-girl

6

22
Rust
The Queen of the Fishes
1894

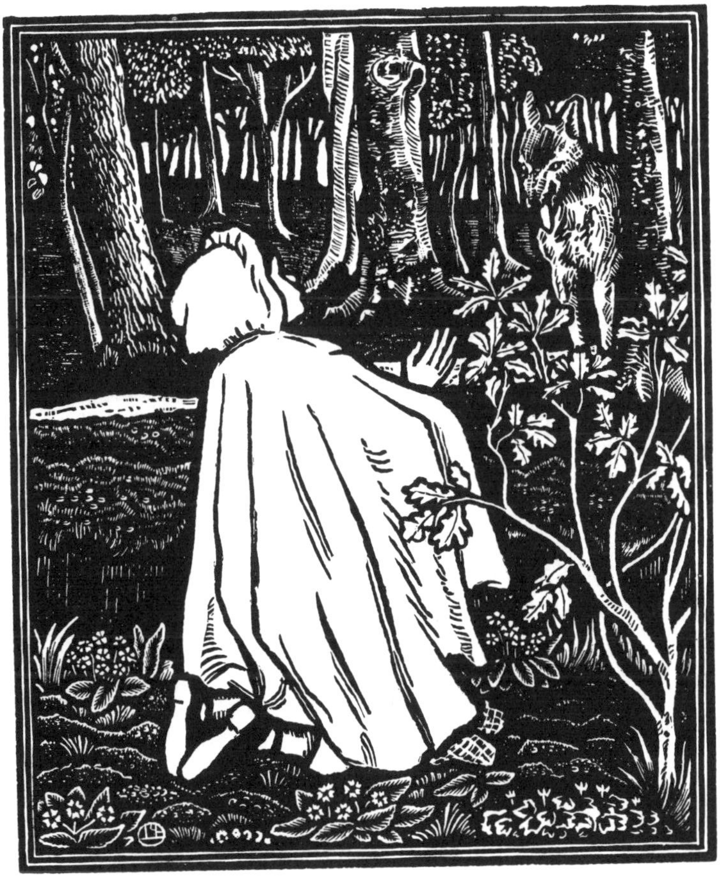

23
Le Petit Chaperon Rouge
c. 1895

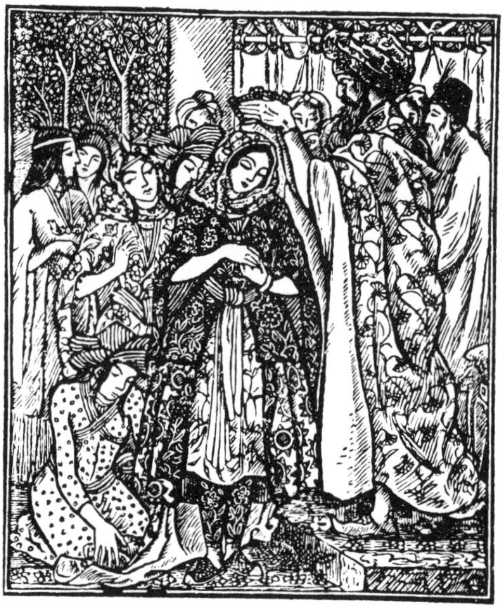

24
The Book of Ruth
1896

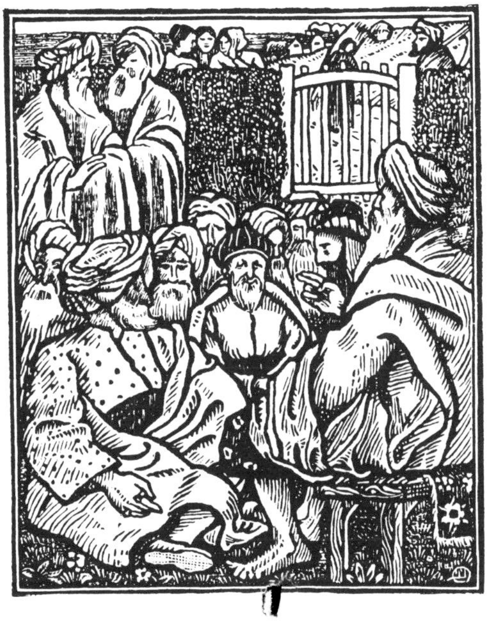

25
The Book of Ruth
1896

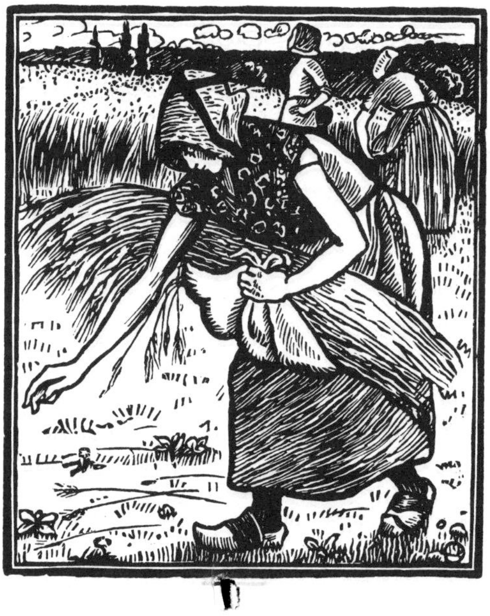

26
The Book of Ruth
1896

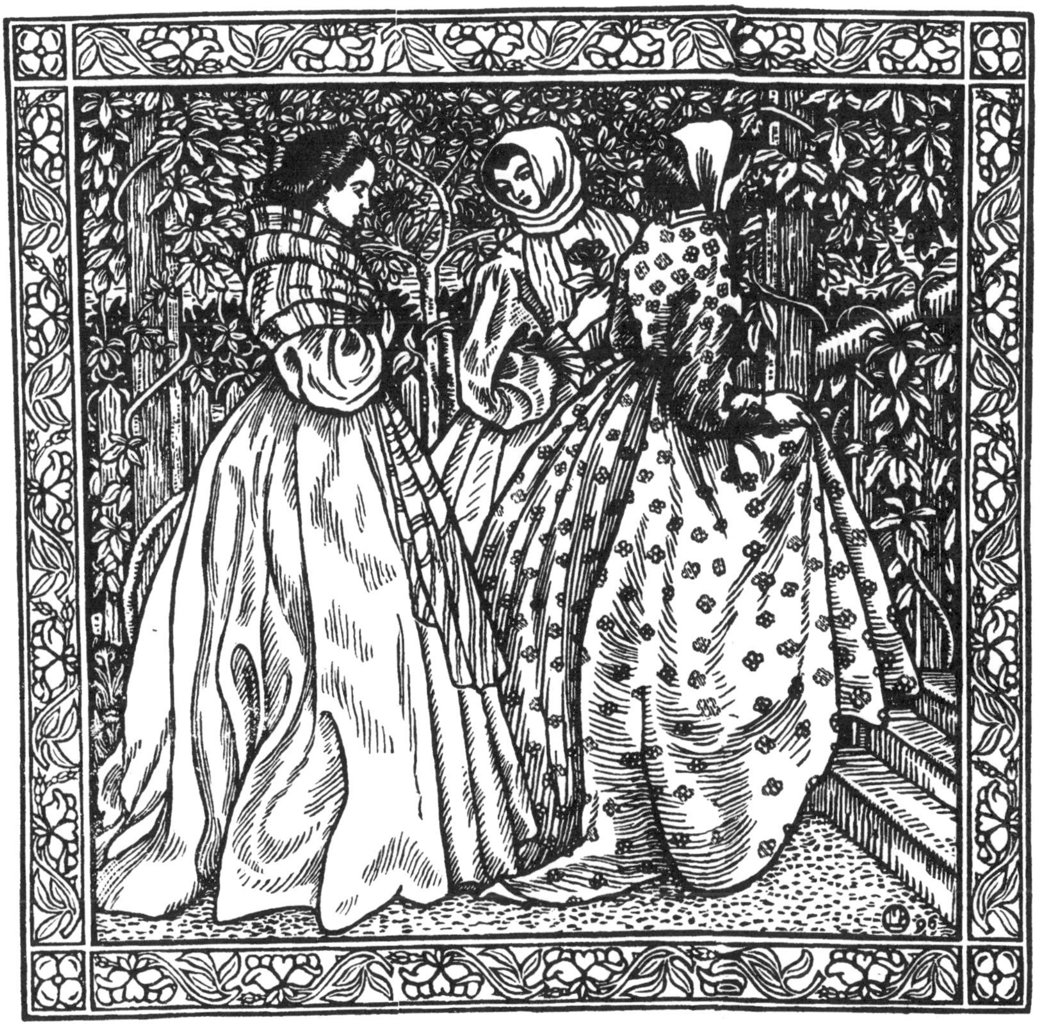

27
Les Roses d'Antan
1896

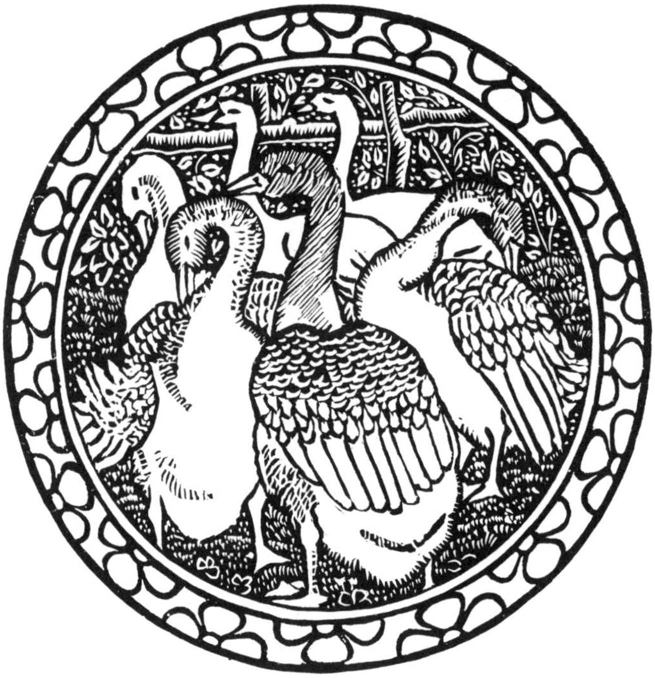

28
Geese
1899

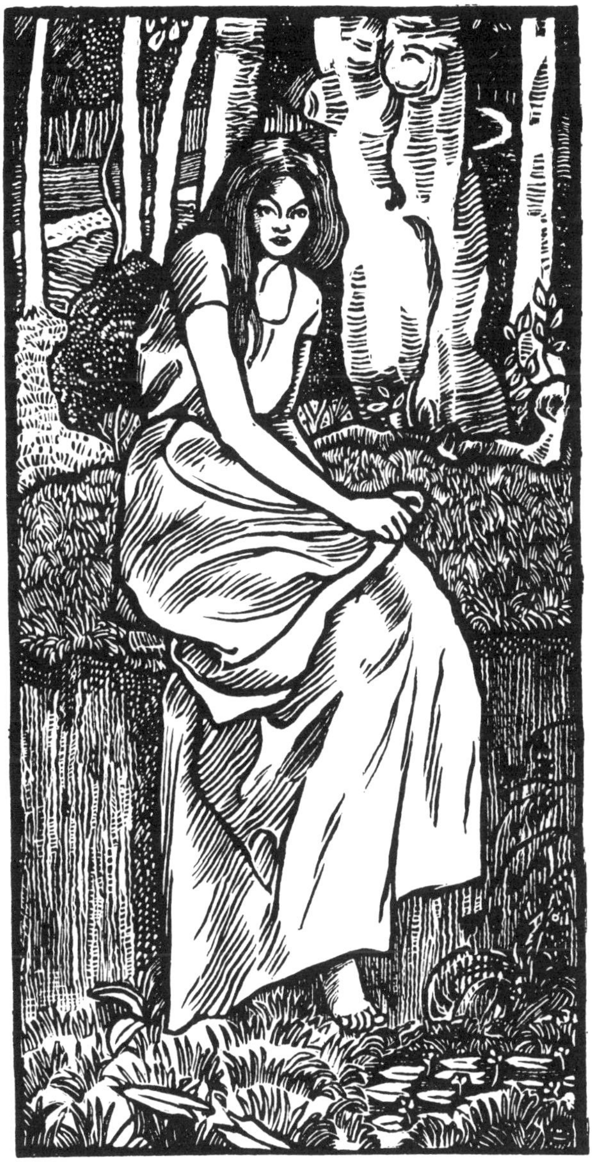

29
Woodland Girl
c. 1899

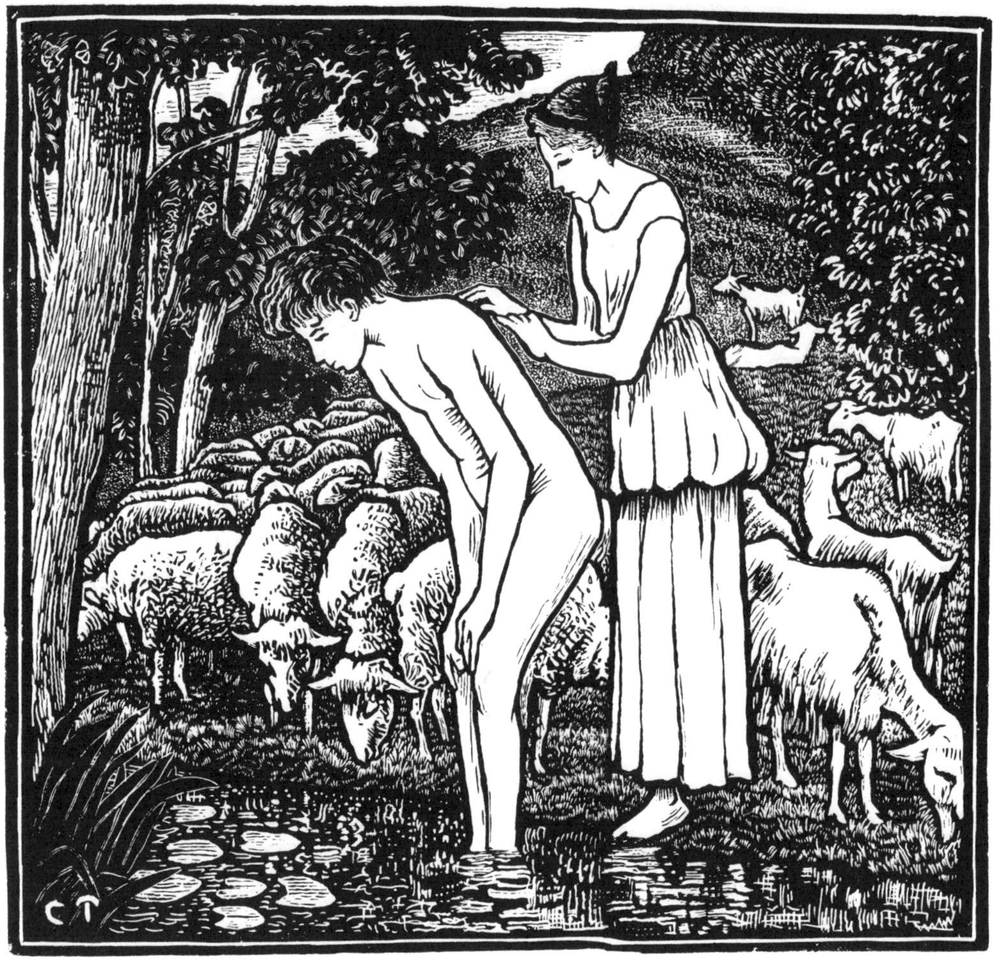

30
Daphnis et Chloë
c. 1899

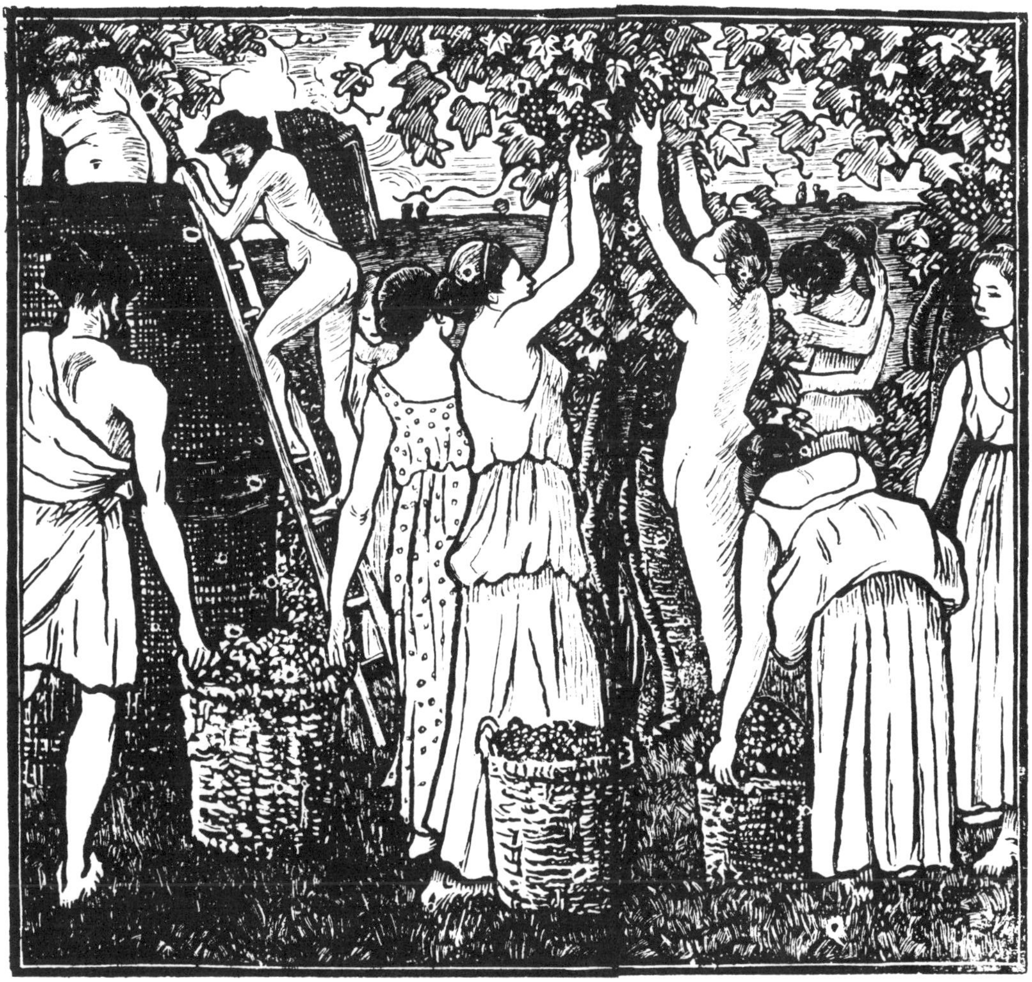

31
Daphnis et Chloë
c. 1899

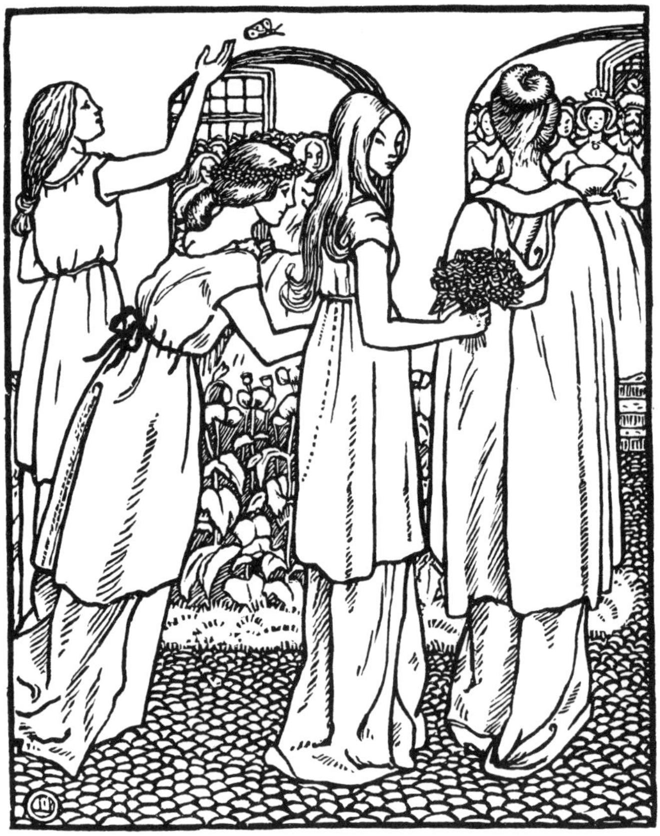

32
Perrault
Deux Contes de ma Mère l'Oye
1899

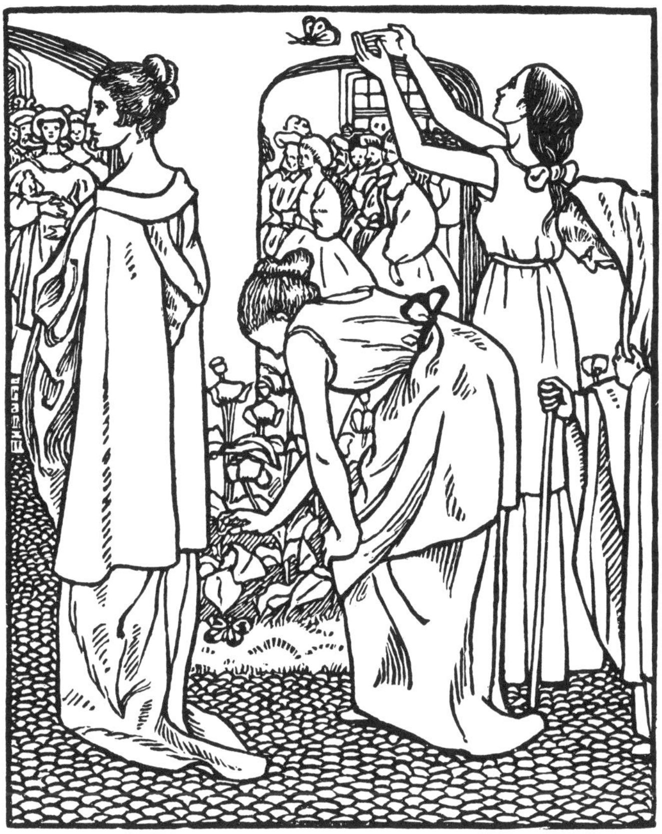

33
Perrault
Deux Contes de ma Mère l'Oye
1899

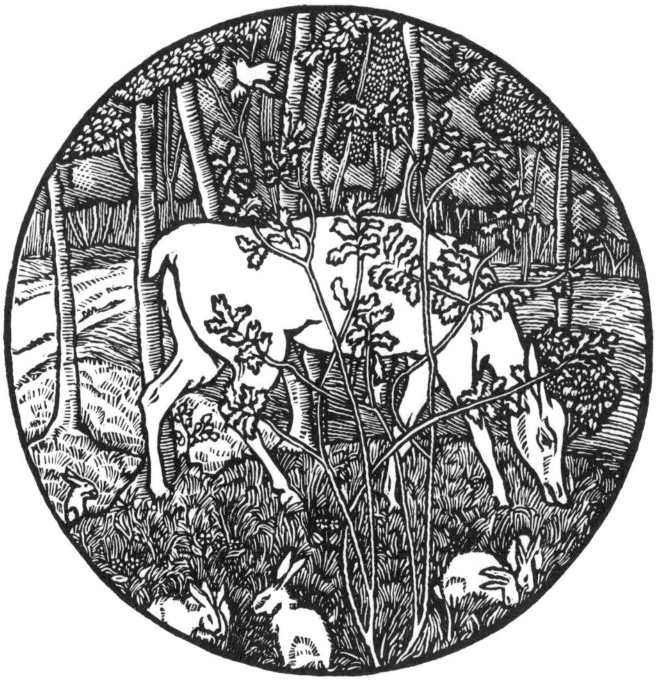

34
Flaubert
La Légende de St. Julien l'Hospitalier
1900

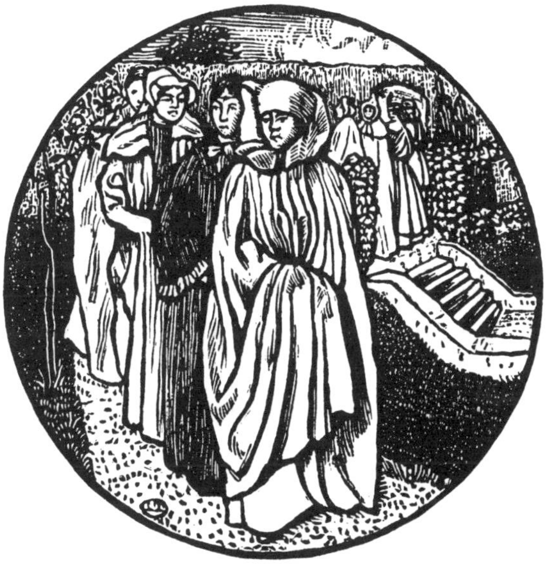

35
Villon
Les Ballades de Maistre François Villon
1900

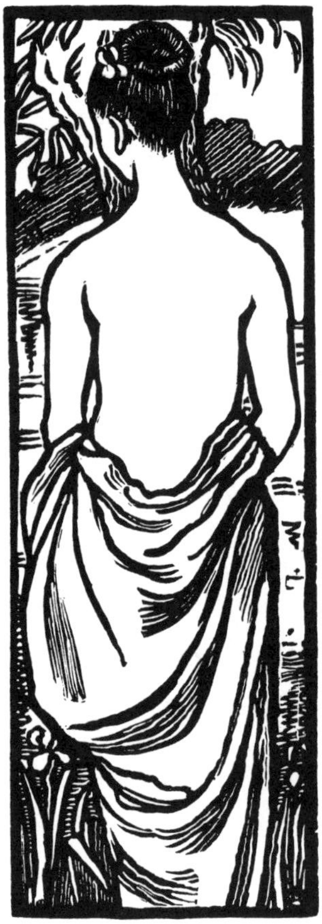

36
Baigneuse
1900

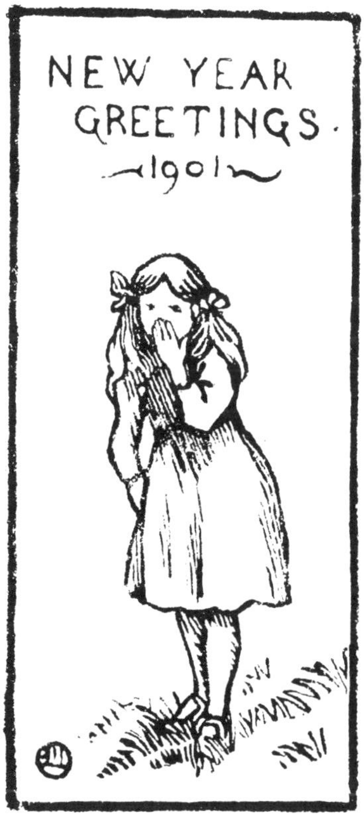

37
New Year Card
1901

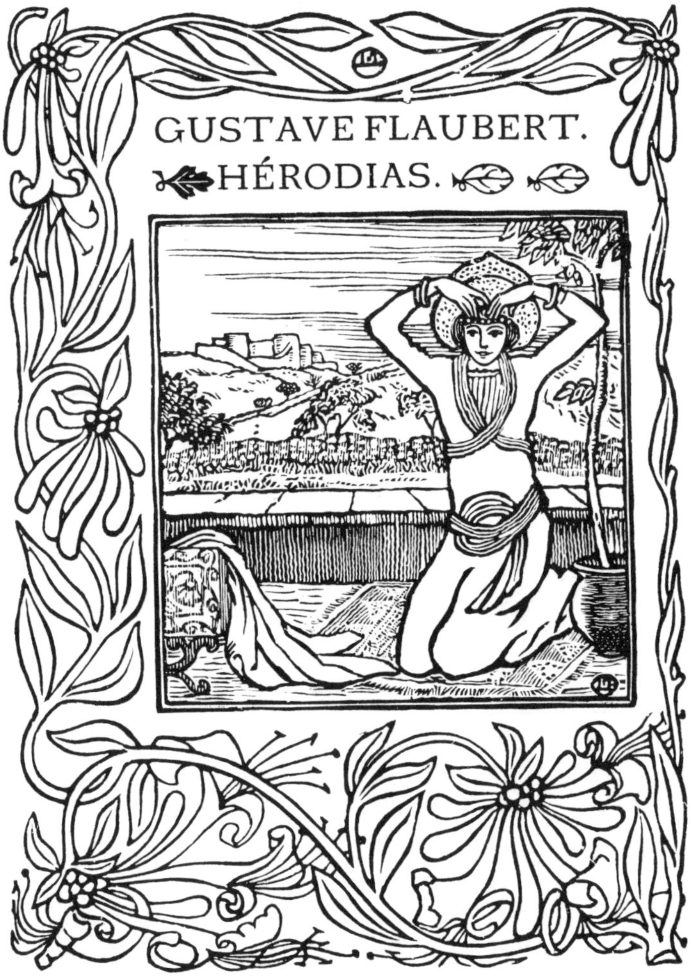

38
Flaubert
Hérodias
1901

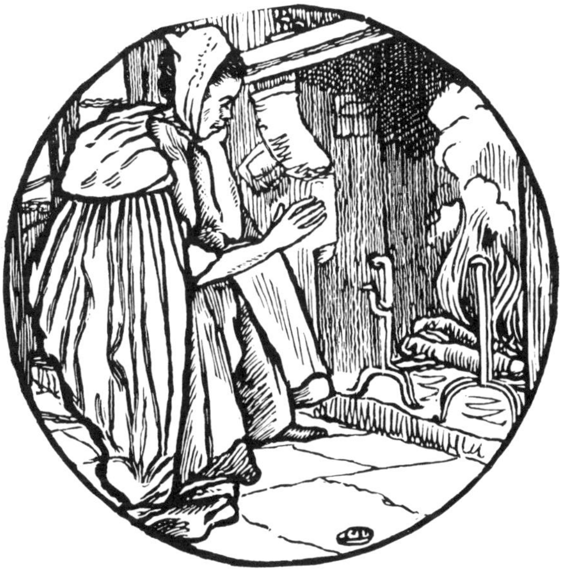

39
Villon
Autres Poésies
1901

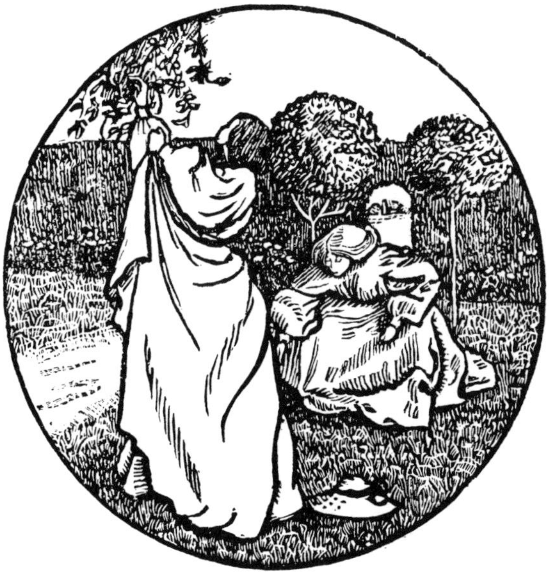

40
Bacon
Of Gardens
1902

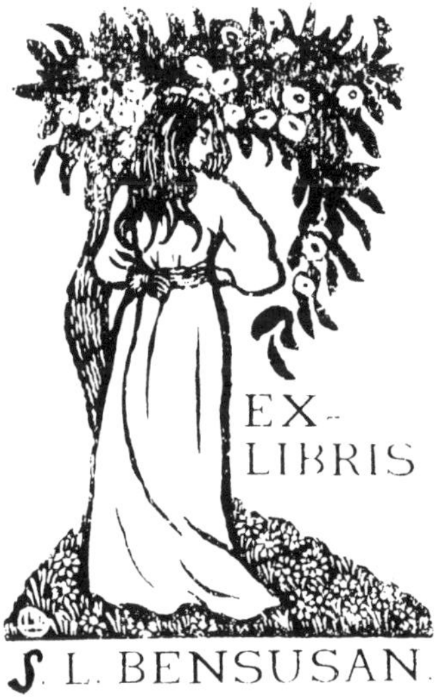

41
Ex Libris
c. 1901

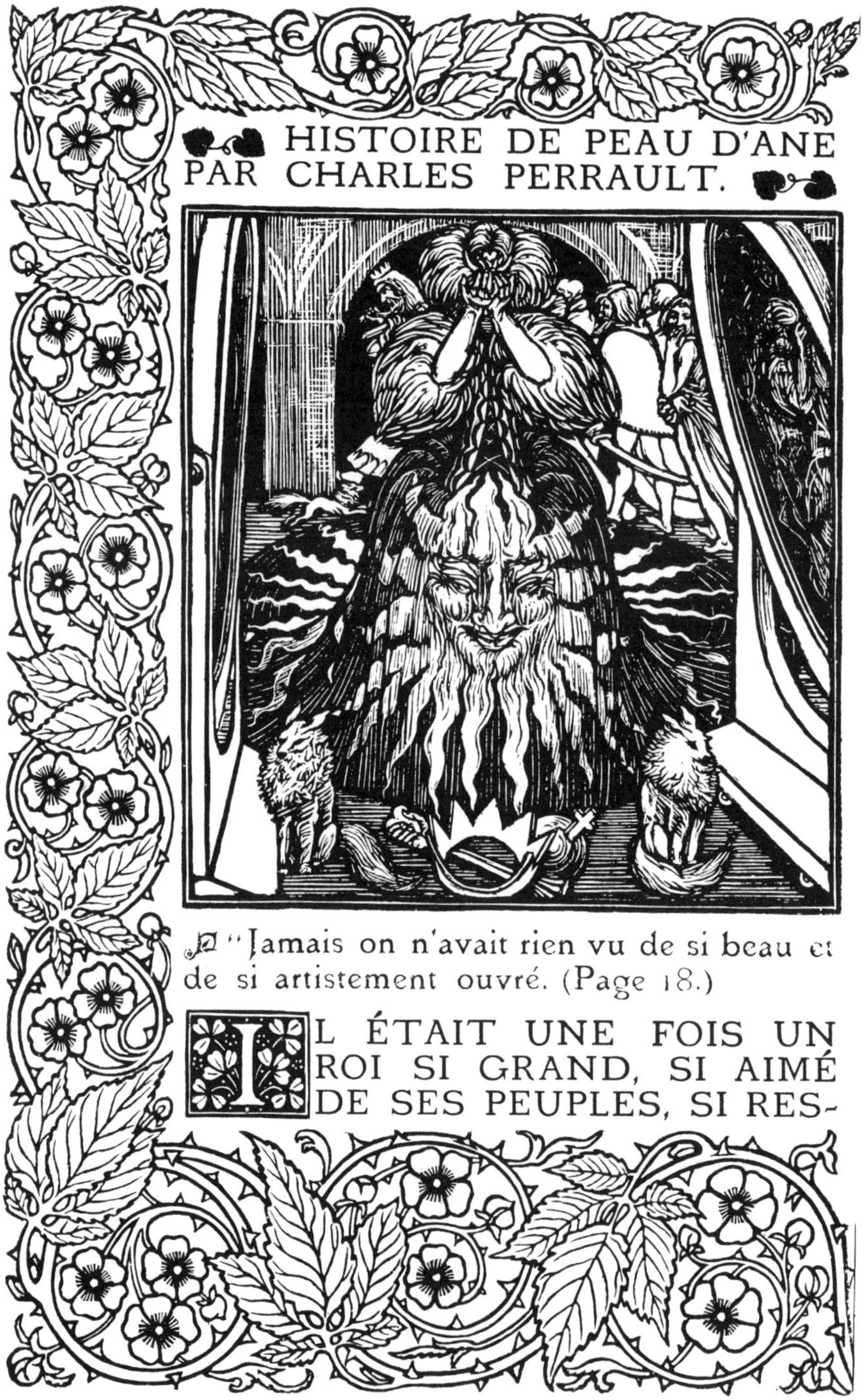

42
Perrault *Histoire de Peau d'Ane*
illustration by T. Sturge Moore
1902

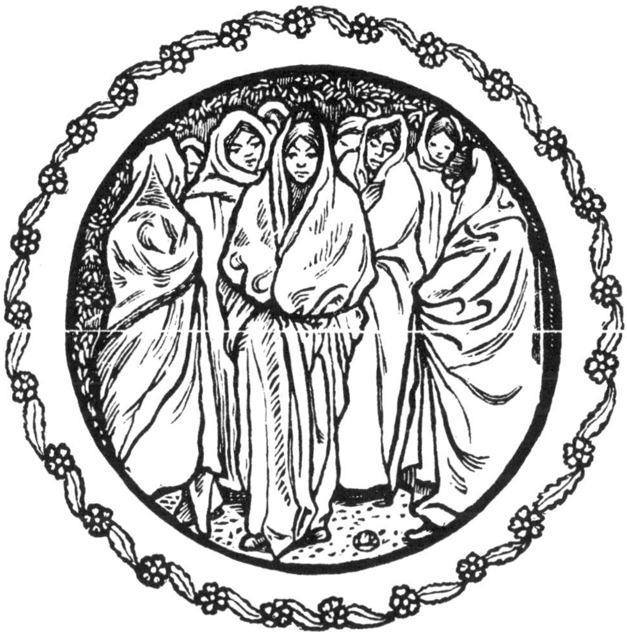

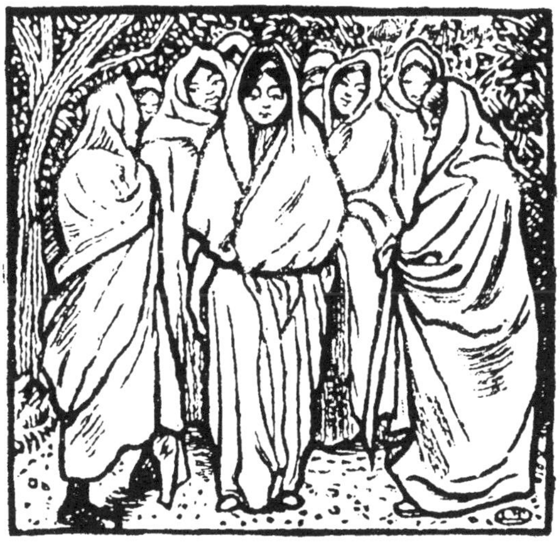

43
Consultation
1905

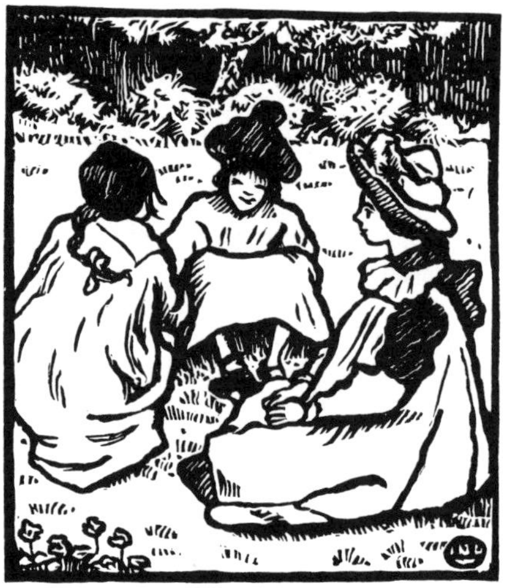

44
Girls sitting on the grass
1906

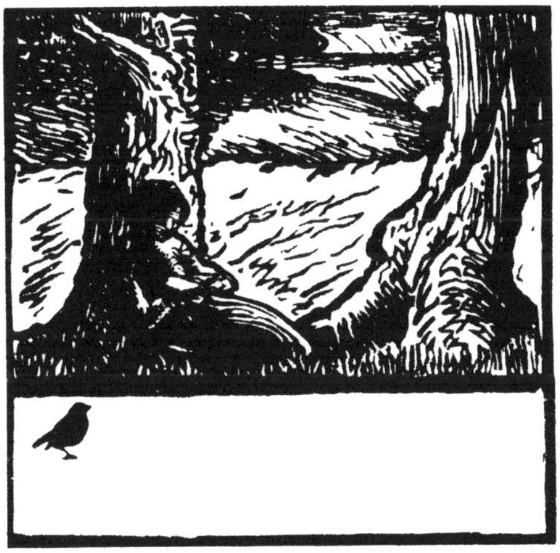

45
Bookplate & New Year card
1905

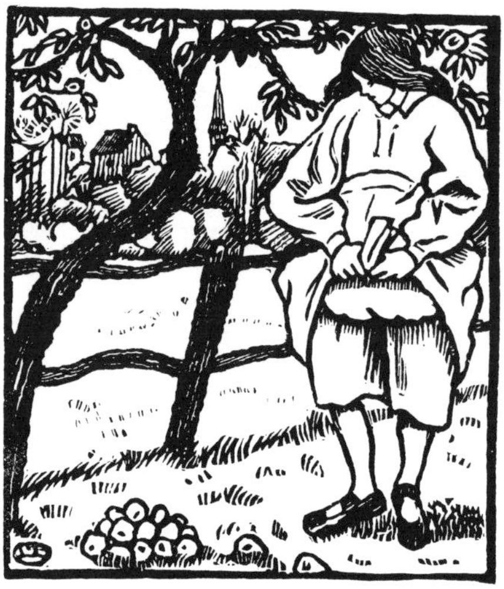

46
Boy gathering apples
1905

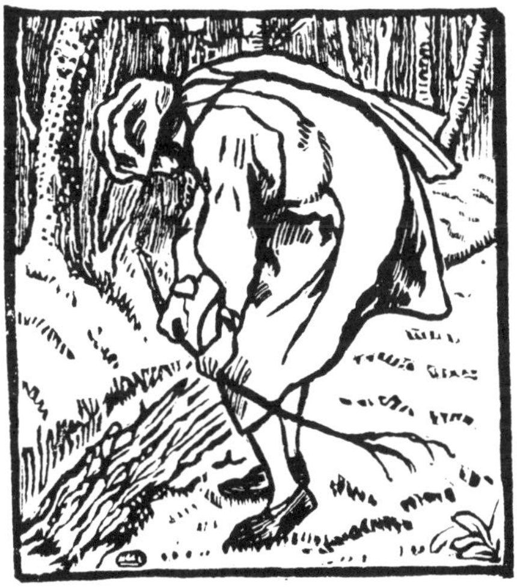

47
Man breaking a stick
1905

VERSES BY CHRISTINA G. ROSSETTI.
DEDICATED TO HER MOTHER.

Perchè temer degg'io? Son le mie voci
Inesperte, lo so: ma il primo omaggio
D'accettarne la MADRE
Perciò non sdegnerà; ch' anzi assai meglio
Quanto a lei grata io sono
L'umil dirà semplicità del dono.

Metastasio.

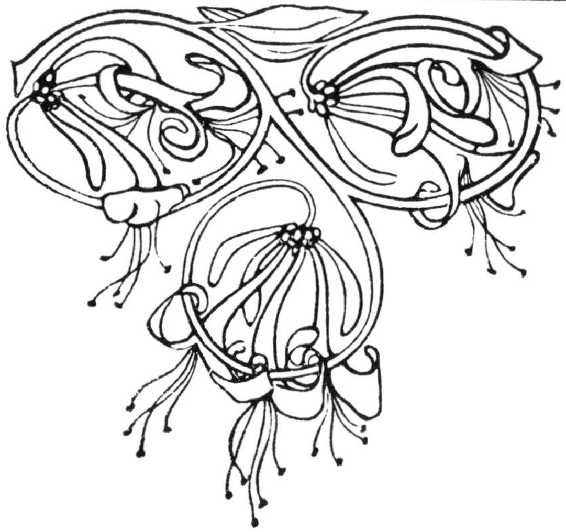

Privately printed at G. Polidori's, No. 15 Park Village East, Regent's Park, London. 1847.

48
Verses by Christina G. Rossetti
1906

VERSES BY CHRISTINA G. ROSSETTI

THE DEAD CITY.

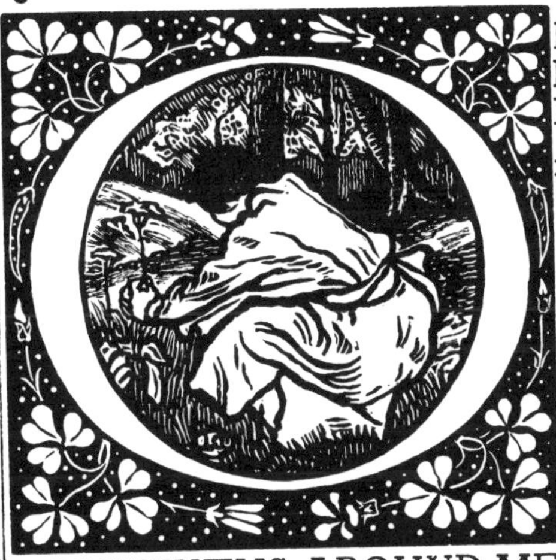

NCE I RAMBLED IN A WOOD
WITH A CARELESS HARDIHOOD
HEEDING NOT THE TANGLED WAY;
LABYRINTHS AROUND ME LAY,
BUT FOR THEM I NEVER STOOD.

On, still on, I wandered on,
And the sun above me shone;
And the birds around me winging
With their everlasting singing
Made me feel not quite alone.

In the branches of the trees
Murmured like the hum of bees
The low sound of happy breezes,
Whose sweet voice that never ceases
Lulls the heart to perfect ease.

49
Verses by Christina G. Rossetti
1906

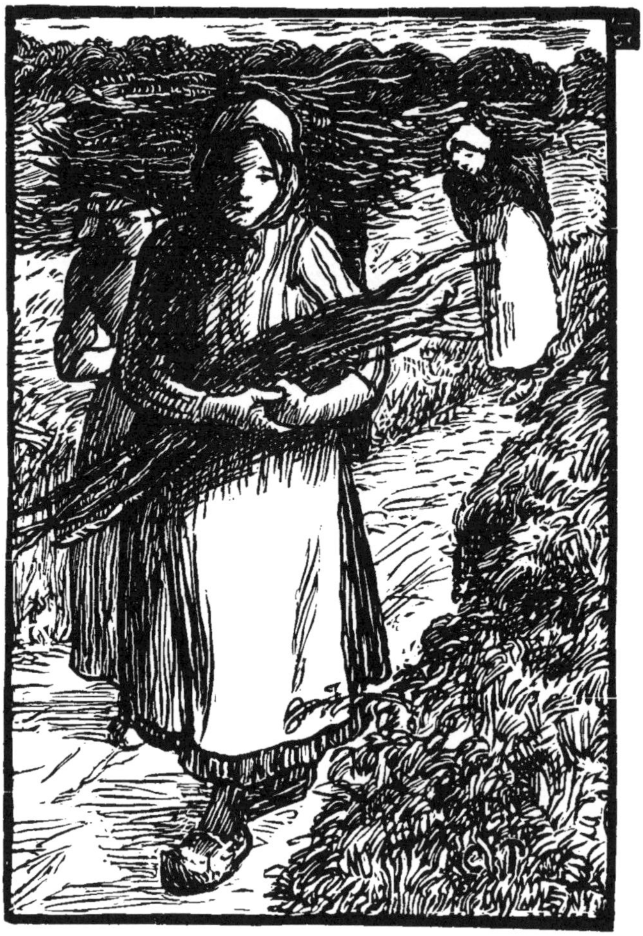

50
Porteuses de Fagot, after Camille Pissarro
1908

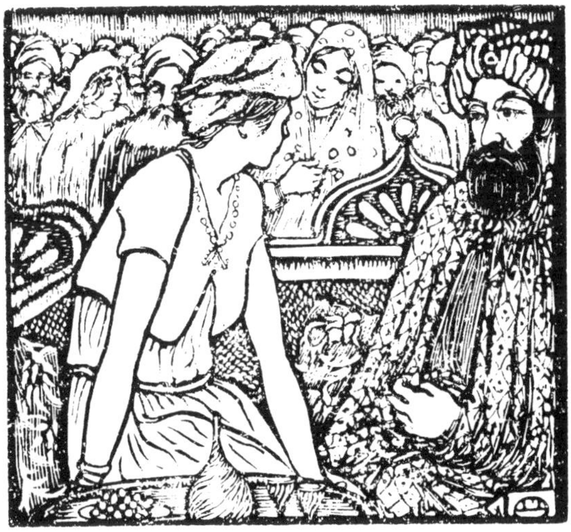

51
Nerval
Histoire de la Reine du Matin et Soliman Ben Daoud
1909

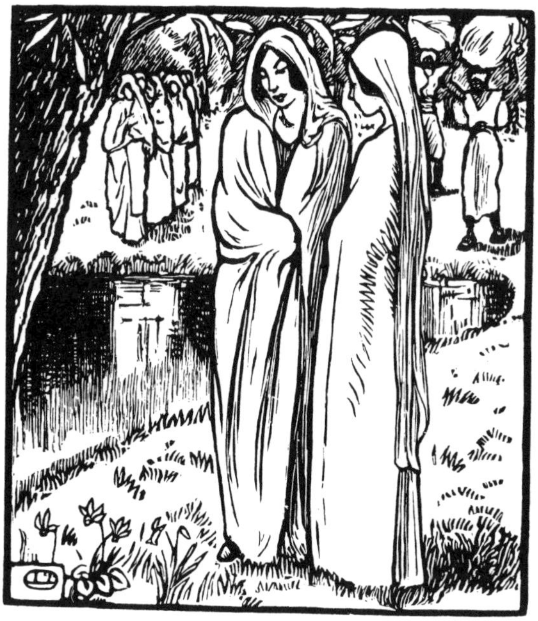

52
Nerval
Histoire de la Reine du Matin et Soliman Ben Daoud
1909

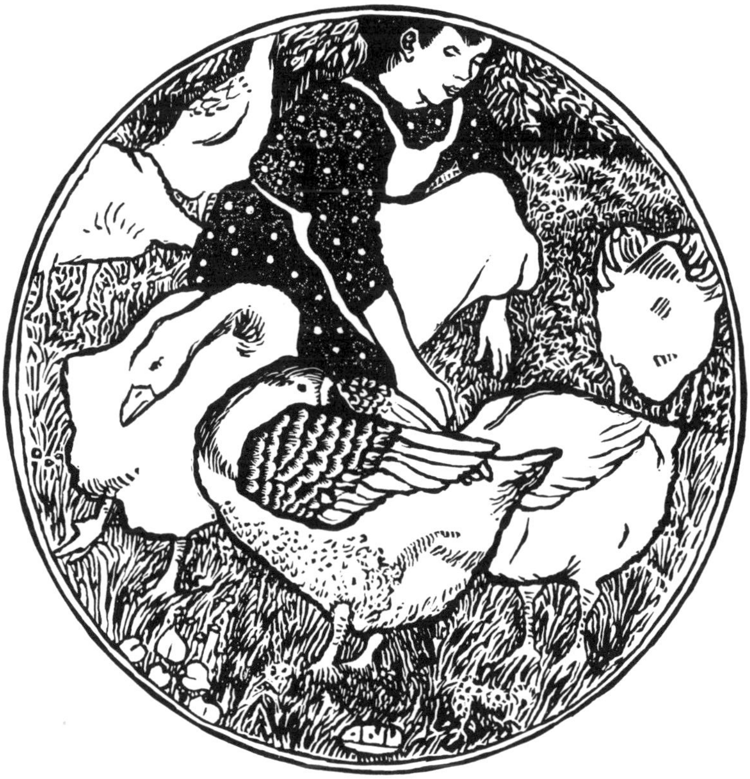

53
Gardeuse d'Oies
1923

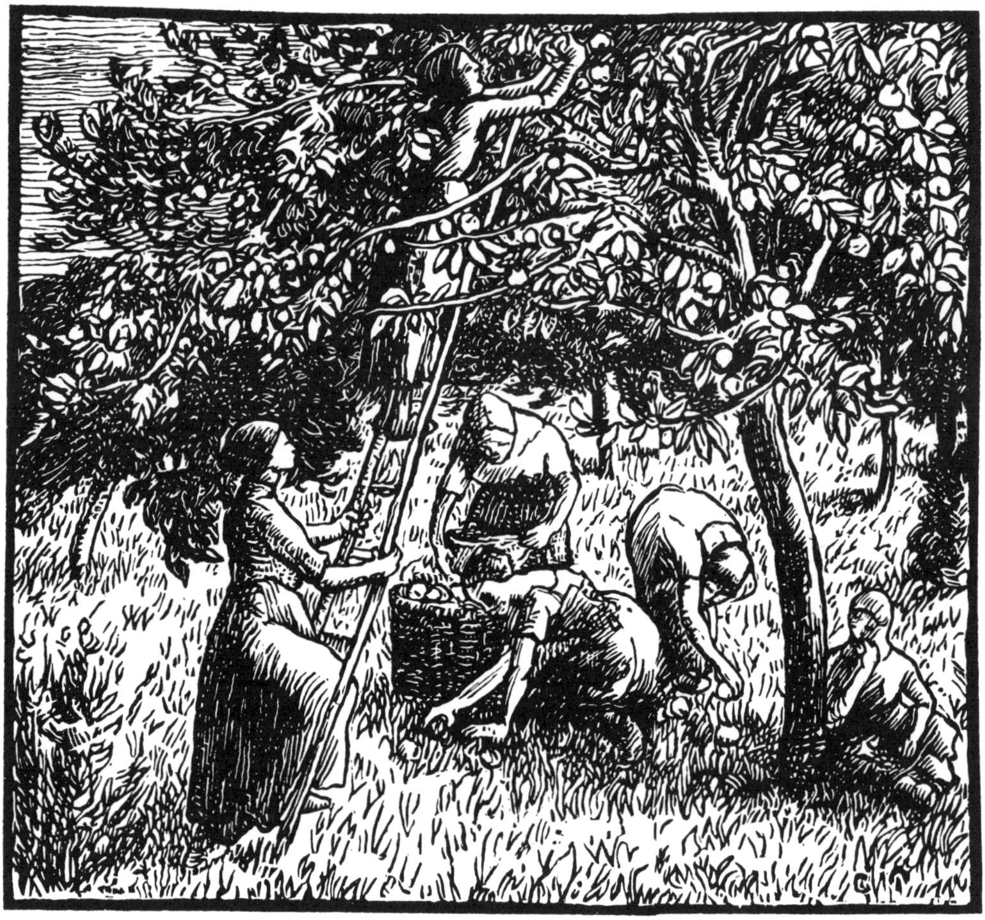

54
Recolte des Pommes, after Camille Pissarro
1925

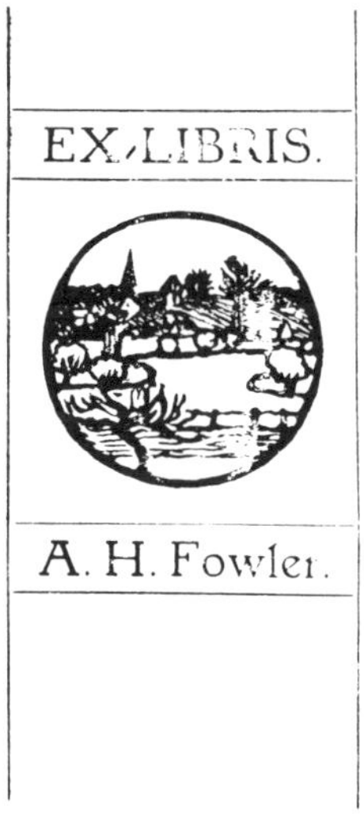

55
Ex libris; View of Eragny, 1892
also A. H. Fowler and in Keats
La Belle Dame Sans Merci
1906

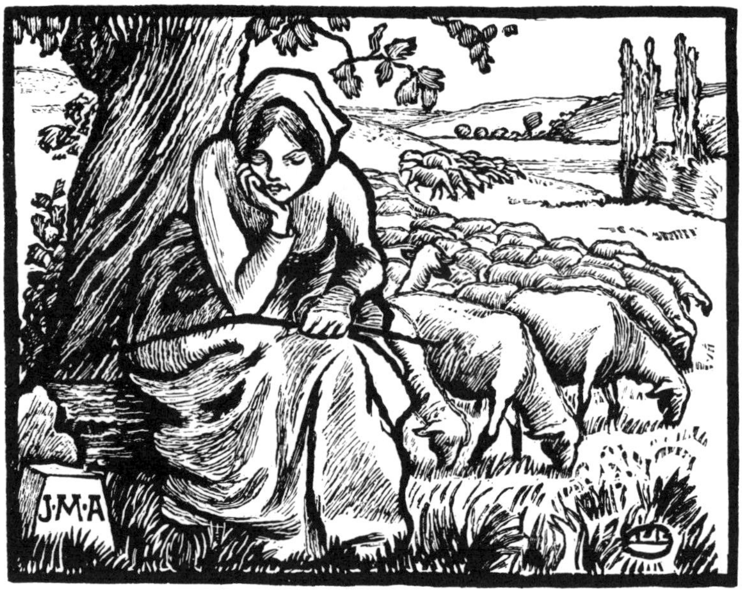

56
Ex libris J. M. Andreini
1907

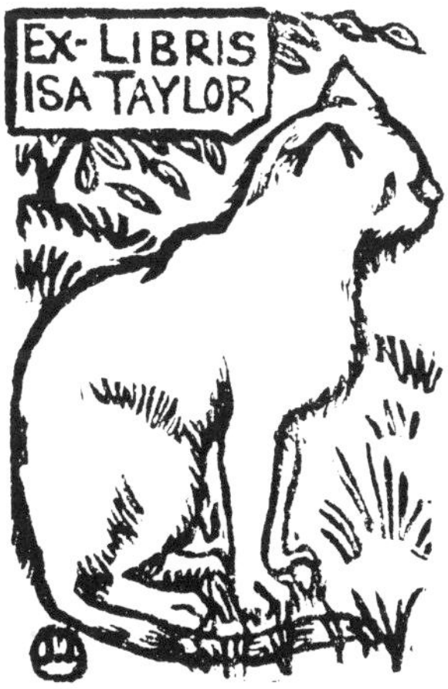

57
Ex libris Isa Taylor
n.d.

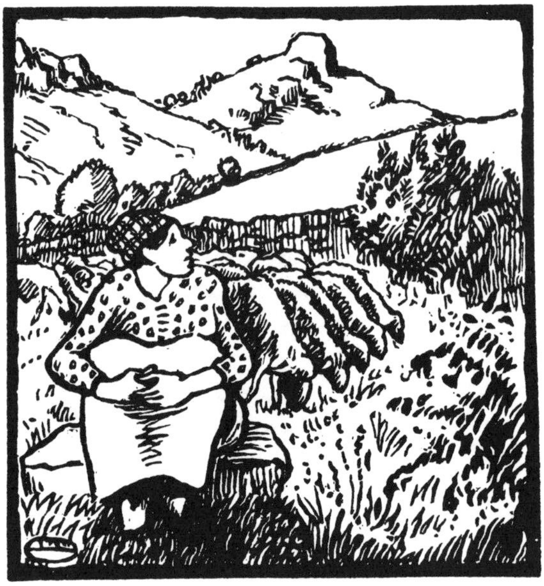

58
La Bergère, Mont Touris
1929

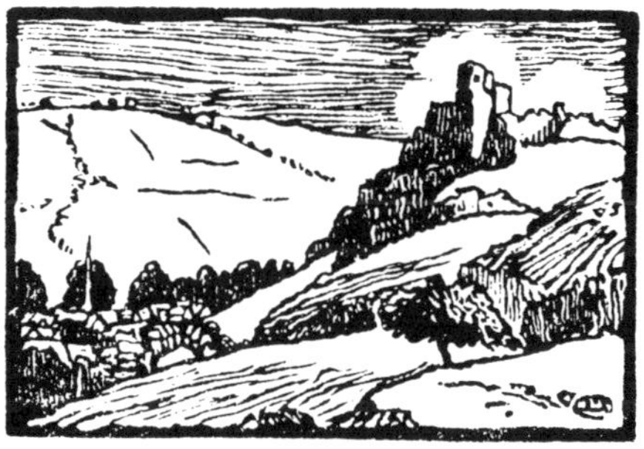

ALL BEST WISHES
FOR THE NEW YEAR
M.CM.XXIV.
FROM
ESTHER, OROVIDA
AND LUCIEN PISSARRO.
The Brook, Stamford Brook,
LONDON.
W. 6.

59
Christmas Card
1924

MCM.XXV.

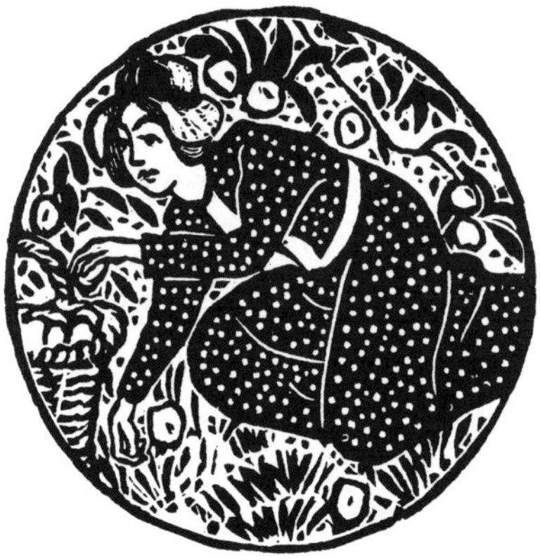

A. ISAACSON SENDS
EVERY GOOD WISH
FOR A HAPPY
XMAS.

9 Aldridge Road Villas. W.11

60
Christmas Card
1925

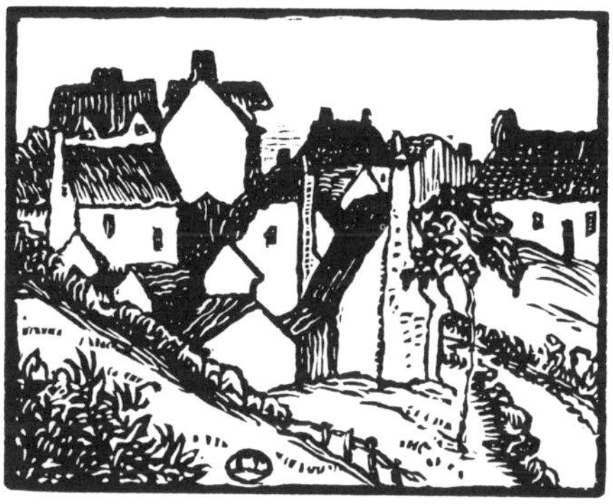

ALL BEST WISHES
FOR THE NEW YEAR
M.CM.XXVII.
FROM
ESTHER, OROVIDA
AND LUCIEN PISSARRO.

The Brook, Stamford Brook,
LONDON.
W. 6.

61
Christmas Card
1927

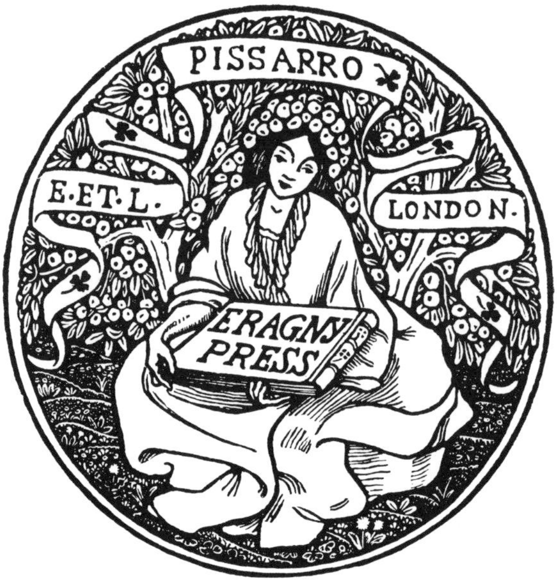

62
Pressmark
1899

CHRONOLOGICAL LIST OF

ERAGNY PRESS BOOKS

Rust, Margaret. *The Queen of the Fishes*. London: Eragny Press / Vale Publications, 1894. Edition 150.

Old Testament. *The Book of Ruth and the Book of Esther*. London: Eragny Press / Sold by Hacon and Ricketts, 1896. Edition 155.

Laforgue, Jules (1860–1887). *Moralités Légendaires*, Vol. I. London: Eragny Press / Sold by Hacon and Ricketts, 1897. Edition 220.

Laforgue, Jules (1860–1887). *Moralités Légendaires*, Vol. II. London: Eragny Press / Sold by Hacon and Ricketts, 1898. Edition 220.

Perrault, Charles (1628–1703). *Deux Contes de ma Mère l'Oye–La Belle au Bois Dormant et Le Petit Chaperon Rouge*. London: Eragny Press / Sold by Hacon and Ricketts, 1899. Edition 224.

Flaubert, Gustave (1821–1880). *La Légende de St. Julien l'Hospitalier*. London: Eragny Press / Sold by Hacon and Ricketts, 1900. Edition 226.

Villon, François (b. 1431). *Les Ballades de Maistre François Villon*. London: Eragny Press / Sold by Hacon and Ricketts, 1900. Edition 226.

Flaubert, Gustave (1821–1880). *Un Cœur Simple*. London: Eragny Press / Sold by Hacon and Ricketts, 1901. Edition 226.

Flaubert, Gustave (1821–1880). *Hérodias*. London: Eragny Press / Sold by Hacon and Ricketts, 1901. Edition 226.

Villon, François (b. 1431). *Autres Poésies de Maistre François Villon et Son Ecole*. London: Eragny Press / Sold by Hacon and Ricketts, 1901. Edition 226.

Verhaeren, Emile (1855–1916). *Les Petits Vieux*. London: Eragny Press / Sold by Hacon and Ricketts, 1901. Edition 230.

Bacon, Francis (1561–1626). *Of Gardens. An Essay*. London: Eragny Press / Sold by Hacon and Ricketts, 1902. Edition 226.

Ronsard, Pierre de (1524–1585). *Choix de Sonnets*. London: Eragny Press / Sold by Hacon and Ricketts, 1902. Edition 226.

Perrault, Charles (1628–1703). *Histoire de Peau d'Ane*. London: Eragny Press / Sold by Hacon and Ricketts, 1902. Edition 230.

Ronsard, Pierre de (1524–1585). *Abrégé de l'Art Poétique Français*. London: Eragny Press / Sold by Hacon and Ricketts, 1903. Edition 226.

C'est d'Aucassin et de Nicolete. London: Eragny Press / Sold by Hacon and Ricketts, 1903. Edition 230.

Moore, Thomas Sturge (1870–1944). *A Brief Account of the Origin of the Eragny Press and a Note on the Relation of the Printed Book as a Work of Art to Life*. Hammersmith: The Eragny Press, 1903. Edition 241.

White, Diana. *The Descent of Ishtar*. Hammersmith: The Eragny Press, 1903. Edition 226.

Milton, John (1608–1674). *Areopagitica*. 1st edition. Hammersmith: The Eragny Press, 1903. Edition 236.

Milton, John (1608–1674). *Areopagitica*. 2nd edition. Hammersmith: The Eragny Press, 1904. Edition 160.

Browning, Robert (1812–1889). *Some Poems by Robert Browning*. Hammersmith: The Eragny Press, 1904. Edition 226.

Coleridge, Samuel Taylor (1772–1834). *Christabel, Kubla Khan, Fancy in Nubibus, and Song from Zapolya*. Hammersmith: The Eragny Press, 1904. Edition 236.

Steele, Robert, editor. *Some Old French and English Ballads*. Hammersmith: The Eragny Press, 1905. Edition 210.

Binyon, Laurence (1869–1943). *Dream Come True*. Hammersmith: The Eragny Press, 1905. Edition 185.

Moore, Thomas Sturge (1870–1944). *The Little School, a Posy of Rhymes*. Hammersmith: The Eragny Press, 1905. Edition 185.

Keats, John (1795–1821). *La Belle Dame sans Merci*. Hammersmith: The Eragny Press, 1906. Edition 210.

Jonson, Ben (1573–1637). *Songs by Ben Jonson. A Selection from the Plays, Masques, and Poems, with the Earliest Known Settings of Certain Numbers.* Hammersmith: The Eragny Press, 1906. Edition 185.

Rossetti, Christina G. (1830–1894). *Verses by Christina G. Rossetti.* Hammersmith: The Eragny Press, 1906. Edition 185.

Perrault, Charles (1628–1703). *Riquet a la Houppe.* Hammersmith: The Eragny Press, 1907. Edition 88.

Nerval, Gérard de (1808–1855). *Histoire de la Reine du Matin et de Soliman Ben Daoud.* Hammersmith: Eragny Press / Paris: Société des Cent Bibliophiles, 1909. Edition 130.

Gautier, Judith (1845–1917). *Poems Tirés du Livre de Jade.* Hammersmith: The Eragny Press, 1911. Edition 130.

Moselly, Emile [pseud. Chénin, Emile] (1870–1918). *La Charrue d'Erable.* Hammersmith: Eragny Press / Paris: Le Livre Contemporain, 1912. Edition 116.

Field, Michael (Katharine Harris Bradley & Edith Emma Cooper). *Whym Chow: Flame of Love.* Hammersmith: The Eragny Press, 1914. Edition 27.

SELECTED BIBLIOGRAPHY

Arts Council of Great Britain. *Lucien Pissarro 1863–1944*. London: Arts Council of Great Britain, 1963.

———. Introduction by Philip James. *Exhibition of Designs and Wood-engravings for the Eragny Press* 1894–1914. London: Arts Council of Great Britain, 1950 (?).

Ashmolean Museum. *Lucien Pissarro: Wood Engravings (29 prints printed from the original blocks now at the Ashmolean)*. Oxford: Ashmolean Museum, 1981.

Bailly-Herzberg, Janine. *Correspondance de Camille Pissarro*. 5 Vols. Presses Universitaires de France, 1980–1991.

Bass, Jacquelynn and Field, Richard. *The Artistic Revival of the Woodcut in France 1850–1900*. Ann Arbor: University of Michigan Museum of Art, 1984.

Bensusan, Samuel Levy. "The Eragny Press." *Booklover's Magazine*, Edinburgh 8 (1908–09): 119–125.

Bensusan-Butt, John. *Recollections of Lucien Pissarro in His Seventies*. London: Anthony d'Offay Gallery, 1977.

———. *The Eragny Press*, 1894–1914. Colchester, England: By the Author, 1975.

Bowness, Alan and Laughton, Bruce. *Decade* 1890–1900. Arts Council of Great Britain: Shenval Press, 1967.

Cave, Roderick. *The Private Press*. 2nd ed. New York & London: Bowker & Co., 1983.

Chambers, David. *Lucien Pissarro: Notes on Selection of Wood Blocks Held at the Ashmolean*. Oxford: Ashmolean Museum, 1980.

Clément-Janin. "Lucien Pissarro: Peintres-graveurs contemporains." *Gazette des Beaux-arts*, 15 (1919): 337–51.

Darracott, Joseph. *The World of Charles Ricketts*. London: Cameron and Tayleur, Ltd., 1980.

Fern, Alan, ed. *Lucien Pissarro: Notes on the Eragny Press and Letter to J.B. Manson* (Cambridge Press Book). Cambridge: Cambridge University Press, 1957.

———. "The Wood-engravings of Lucien Pissarro, with a Catalogue Raisonné." PhD. dissertation, University of Chicago, 1960.

Findlay Galleries. *Lucien Pissarro*. New York: Findlay Galleries, 1966.

Franklin, Colin. *The Private Presses*. 2nd ed. England and Vermont: Scolar Press & Gower Publishing Co., 1991.

Garvey, Eleanor M. "Art Nouveau and the French Books of the Eighteen-Nineties." *Harvard Library Bulletin*, XII (1958): 375–391.

Genz, Marcella D. "The History of the Eragny Press 1894–1914." PhD. dissertation, University of California, Berkeley, 1990.

Houghton Library, introduction by Peter A. Wick. *The Turn of a Century: Art Nouveau-Jugendstil Books*. Cambridge: Harvard University Dept. of Printing & Graphic Arts, 1970.

Hutton, John. "Les Prolos Vagabondent: Neo-Impressionism and the Anarchist Image of the Trimardeur." *Art Bulletin*, 72 (June 1990): 296–309.

Jackson, Holbrook. *Private Presses in England*. Philadelphia: Lanston Monotype Machine Co., 1923.

Johnson, Una E. *Ambroise Vollard Editeur: 1867–1939. An Appreciation and Catalogue*. New York: Wittenborn and Co., 1944.

Manson, John Bolivar. "Notes on some wood-engravings of Lucien Pissarro." *The Imprint*, London (April 17, 1913): 240–247.

McLean, Ruari. *Modern Book Design from William Morris to the Present Day*. London: Faber & Faber, 1958.

Meadmore, William Sutton. *Lucien Pissarro, Un Cœur Simple*. London, 1962.

Nicolson, Benedict. "The Anarchism of Camille Pissarro." *The Arts*, London, 2 (1947): 43–51.

"Note on Lucien Pissarro." *L'Art Moderne*, Brussels, (6 August 1893).

Perkins, Geoffrey. *The Gentle Art*. Zurich: L'Art Ancien, 1974.

Rewald, John. "Lucien Pissarro. Letters from London, 1883–1891." *Burlington Magazine*, XCI (1949): 188ff.

———, editor, with the assistance of Lucien Pissarro. *Camille Pissarro: Letters to His Son Lucien*. New York: Pantheon Books Inc., 1943.

Ricketts, Charles and Pissarro, Lucien. *De la Typogpraphie et de l'Harmonie de la Page Imprimée: William Morris et son influence sur la arts et métiers*. London: Vale Press, 1898.

———, and Shannon, Charles. *The Dial (an Occasional Publication)* Vols. I–V. London: Ballantyne Press / Hacon and Ricketts, 1889–1896.

Robb, Brian. "The Wood-engravings of Lucien Pissarro." *Signature*, n.s. 6 (1948): 36f.

Roberts, W. "The Print Room, British Museum, Lucien Pissarro." *Magazine of Art*, XXVI (1902): 276–278.

Rose, Jonathan and Anderson, Patricia J., editors. *British Literary Publishing Houses, 1881–1965. Vol. 112: Dictionary of Literary Biography*. Detroit/London: Bruccoli Clark Layman Book, Gale Research Inc., 1991.

Rothenstein, William. *Men and Memories: Recollections of William Rothenstein, 1872–1900*. New York: Coward-McCann, Inc., 1931.

Salaman, Malcolm C. *British Book Illustration Yesterday and To-day*. London: The Studio, Ltd., 1923.

Stetz, Margaret D. and Lasner, Mark Samuels. *England in the 1890s: Literary Publishing at the Bodley Head*. Washington, D.C.: Georgetown University Press, 1990.

Symons, Arthur J.A. "An Unacknowledged Movement in Fine Printing, the Typography of the Eighteen-Nineties." *The Fleuron*, VII (1930): 83–119.

Taylor, John Russell. *The Art Nouveau Book in Britain*. Cambridge, MA: MIT Press, 1966.

Thorold, Anne. "The Pissarro Collection in the Ashmolean Museum, Oxford." *Burlington Magazine* (October 1978).

———. *Catalogue of Oil Paintings of Lucien Pissarro*. London: Athelney Books, 1983.

———, editor. *Letters of Lucien to Camille Pissarro, 1883–1903*. Volume in *Cambridge Studies in the History of Art*. Cambridge: Cambridge University Press, 1993.

———. *Pissarro: Monde Rural—Art—Politique*. Exhibition Catalogue: Centre Cultural du Marais, 4 fev—26 avril, 1981.

Vollard, Ambroise. *Recollections of a Picture Dealer*. New York: Dover Publications, Inc., 1978.

Lora Urbanelli has worked in the museum field for many years, specializing in works of art on paper. She is currently Curator of Prints, Drawings and Photographs at the Museum of Art, Rhode Island School of Design.

The Book Art of Lucien Pissarro was designed and typeset by Wesley B. Tanner at Passim Editions, Ann Arbor, Michigan. The types used were Caxton, Goudy italic, and Schneidler. Fifteen hundred copies were printed at Data Reproductions in Rochester Hills, Michigan on acid-free paper.